S. Hrg. 106–486

CYBER ATTACK: IS THE GOVERNMENT SAFE?

HEARING

BEFORE THE

COMMITTEE ON GOVERNMENTAL AFFAIRS UNITED STATES SENATE

ONE HUNDRED SIXTH CONGRESS

SECOND SESSION

MARCH 2, 2000

Printed for the use of the Committee on Governmental Affairs

U.S. GOVERNMENT PRINTING OFFICE

63–639 cc WASHINGTON : 2000

For sale by the U.S. Government Printing Office
Superintendent of Documents, Congressional Sales Office, Washington, DC 20402

ISBN 0-16-060743-4

COMMITTEE ON GOVERNMENTAL AFFAIRS

FRED THOMPSON, Tennessee, *Chairman*

WILLIAM V. ROTH, Jr., Delaware
TED STEVENS, Alaska
SUSAN M. COLLINS, Maine
GEORGE V. VOINOVICH, Ohio
PETE V. DOMENICI, New Mexico
THAD COCHRAN, Mississippi
ARLEN SPECTER, Pennsylvania
JUDD GREGG, New Hampshire

JOSEPH I. LIEBERMAN, Connecticut
CARL LEVIN, Michigan
DANIEL K. AKAKA, Hawaii
RICHARD J. DURBIN, Illinois
ROBERT G. TORRICELLI, New Jersey
MAX CLELAND, Georgia
JOHN EDWARDS, North Carolina

HANNAH S. SISTARE, *Staff Director and Counsel*
ELLEN B. BROWN, *Senior Counsel*
SUSAN G. MARSHALL, *Professional Staff Member*
JOYCE A. RECHTSCHAFFEN, *Minority Staff Director and Counsel*
DEBORAH COHEN LEHRICH, *Minority Counsel*
DARLA D. CASSELL, *Administrative Clerk*

CONTENTS

CYBER ATTACK: IS THE GOVERNMENT SAFE?

THURSDAY, MARCH 2, 2000

U.S. SENATE,
COMMITTEE ON GOVERNMENTAL AFFAIRS,
Washington, DC.

The Committee met, pursuant to notice, at 10:05 a.m., in room SD–342, Dirksen Senate Office Building, Hon. Fred Thompson, Chairman of the Committee, presiding.

Present: Senators Thompson, Collins, Lieberman, Akaka, and Edwards.

OPENING STATEMENT OF CHAIRMAN THOMPSON

Chairman THOMPSON. The Committee will be in order, please. I am afraid we are going to have a vote. I guess it is on right now, so we will have to leave momentarily, but let us see if we can get a little something accomplished before we have to leave.

Today, the Committee on Governmental Affairs is holding a hearing on the ability of the Federal Government to protect against and respond to potential cyber attacks. This Committee spent considerable time during the last Congress examining the state of Federal Government information systems. Numerous Governmental Affairs Committee hearings and General Accounting Office reports uncovered and identified systemic failures of government information systems, which highlighted our Nation's vulnerability to computer attacks from international and domestic terrorists, to crime rings, to everyday hackers.

We directed GAO to study computer security vulnerabilities at several Federal agencies, including the Internal Revenue Service, the State Department, the Federal Aviation Administration, the Social Security Administration, and the Department of Veterans' Affairs. From these and other numerous reports, we learned that our Nation's underlying information infrastructure is riddled with vulnerabilities which represent severe security flaws and risks to our national security, public safety, and personal privacy.

Every year, the government gathers information on every one of us because we give the government this information in order to obtain government services, like getting Social Security benefits, veterans' benefits, Medicare, or paying taxes, and yet, year after year, this Committee continues to receive reports detailing security breaches at these same agencies. Sometimes these things improve. Agencies usually will respond to specific GAO recommendations or to a particular Inspector General report. But this is a band-aid approach to protecting information systems, that is, fixing the system little by little, problem by problem after it is revealed that it is no longer secure.

What is most alarming to me is that after all this time and all these reports, there is still no organization-wide approach to preventing cyber attacks and the security program management is totally inadequate. I am afraid it is another example of how difficult it is to get the Federal bureaucracy to move even in an area as important as this.

Those reports highlight that an underlying cause of Federal information security vulnerabilities is inadequate security program planning and management. When GAO studied the management practices of eight organizations known for their superior security programs, GAO found that these organizations manage information security through continuous management activities, which included specific practices to support their information security principles. We think this is lacking in the Federal Government.

And we think agencies must do more than establish programs and set management goals. Agencies and the people responsible for information systems in those agencies must be held accountable for their actions, and I believe that Congress should examine how we can provide assistance to the agencies to ensure that they have the resources necessary to maintain information technology security preparedness at all times.

It is clear to me, based on GAO report after GAO report, that what needs to emerge in government is a coordinated and comprehensive management approach to protecting information which incorporates the efforts already underway and takes advantage of the extended amount of evidence that we have gathered over the years. The objective of such an approach should be to encourage agency improvement efforts and measure their effectiveness through an appropriate level of oversight.

In order to develop such an approach and begin to find solutions to the problems which have been identified, we concluded that a more complete statutory foundation for improvement is needed. That is why Senator Lieberman and I introduced S. 1993, the Government Information Security Act, at the end of last year. The primary objective of our bill is to address the management challenges associated with operating in the current interdependent computing environment.

Our bill begins where the Paperwork Reduction Act of 1995 and the Clinger-Cohen Act of 1996 left off. These laws and the Computer Security Act of 1987 provide the basic framework for managing information security. We recognize that these are not the only things that need to be done. Some have suggested we provide specific standards in the legislation. Others have recommended we establish a new position of a national chief information officer or even a national security czar. These things should be considered and these issues and more will be brought up during our hearing today.

The witnesses before us represent a broad array of experience and expertise in the area of information security. First, we have Kevin Mitnick, who has described himself as a reformed hacker.

Next, we will hear from Jack Brock, who is the Director of Governmentwide and Defense Information Systems at GAO, and Roberta Gross, Inspector General for NASA. Both of them have done significant work in the area of Government information security.

We will also hear from Ken Watson, who is the Manager of Critical Infrastructure Protection at Cisco Systems, Inc., and James Adams, the CEO and co-founder of iDEFENSE.

I welcome all of you and look forward to your testimony about the cyber threats that we face today and how we can work together to fashion solutions to the many problems associated with computer security.

Senator Lieberman.

OPENING STATEMENT OF SENATOR LIEBERMAN

Senator LIEBERMAN. Thank you very much, Mr. Chairman. Thanks for calling this hearing on a topic of enormous concern to all of us. The security of our digital information is something that affects every one of us on a daily basis and should be taken as seriously as the security of our property, of our neighborhoods, of our communities, of our Nation, and in the worst case, as seriously as the security of our lives.

The reach of the Internet and the alacrity with which it has achieved that reach is the story of the closing years of the 20th Century and the beginning of the 21st Century. Enabled by the remarkable innovation in information technology, we are fast approaching a time when the world will always be on, always connected, always open for business. It will be a fast environment marked by increasing efficiency and decreased cost. But it also will be intensely competitive and without boundaries. Almost every institution we rely on in our daily lives is feeling the effect of this latest technological revolution.

Just last month, the General Services Administration's Chief Information Officer, Bill Piatt, wrote something that I think all of us in government should keep in mind, "From the perspective of our bosses, the citizens, electronic government is neither an option to be chosen nor a mandate to be decreed. It is simply expected."

So the basic goals of e-Government, which are the electronic delivery of information and services, are the same as government's goals have always been, as enumerated in our Constitution and the laws that we have adopted pursuant to it. But if government is going to be plugged into the networked world as an active permanent presence, we will have to protect the confidentiality, the integrity, and, of course, the availability of the information contained on government computers.

We must be acutely aware of the range and content of the information at stake here. It covers everything from the movements of our armed forces and the deployment of our most powerful weapons to accumulated data about the economy and the financial markets, to support for our transportation networks, to the most private information about the American people, such as tax, wage, and medical records.

The information in far too many cases today is wide open to exploitation, from pranksters to terrorists and every disaffected person in between. The fact that the GAO has labeled as "high risk" virtually the entire computer security system of our government is just unacceptable. We must take action, and quickly, to get the government's computer security systems off of the high-risk watch list.

Last year, Senator Thompson and I, and this Committee, looked into what went wrong in the Federal investigation of Dr. Wen Ho Lee, the former Los Alamos nuclear laboratory scientist who is charged with downloading classified information to an unclassified computer. Mr. Lee has been indicted now. The Justice Department is still investigating other areas and, of course, his guilt or innocence is yet to be determined. But the case should focus everyone's attention on the vulnerability that comes with reliance on computers. So, too, should the more recent revelations of former CIA Director John Deutch, who maintained sensitive information on his home computer.

The hacking of government sites, including those at the Senate, the FBI, the White House, Interior, and the Department of Defense is actually becoming a near daily occurrence, and I would not be surprised if scores of other government sites have also been invaded. But the truth is, we will never know because monitoring intrusions, much less reporting them, is not required.

There are many reasons Federal computer-based information is inadequately protected, but the underlying problem, according to GAO, who we will hear from this morning, is poor management. In some cases, this is a cultural problem. Our concentration on security simply has not grown at the same pace as our reliance on computers. That is why the Government Information Security Act of 1999, which Chairman Thompson and I have introduced, is a beginning step toward correcting this fundamental shortcoming. The bill would put every government agency on notice that it must implement a computer security plan which will be subject to annual independent audits, report unauthorized intrusions, and provide security awareness training for all its workers.

There are a number of areas we have not addressed in our bill yet and we will be asking for input on how best to handle them. For example, the government needs to increase dramatically the number of trained information security professionals. In that regard, I am intrigued by President Clinton's proposal for a Federal Cyberservice at universities based on the ROTC model, and we need incentives for universities to train more people in this area.

We also need to consider what to do to keep the government informed of technological changes in computer security so we do not fall behind. The President's proposal to establish a National Institute for Infrastructure Protection sounds like a good idea if it provides assistance with R&D and technical support.

Mr. Chairman, I am hopeful that the proposal that you and I have made will stimulate significant debate and early action. Our bill is a work in progress. I know that we anticipate hearing from a broad range of interested parties. We have got to particularly listen to those in private industry who have made, I think, much more headway than we in the public sector have in protecting the security of computer-based information, because we do not need to reinvent the wheel here, a very high-tech wheel. We need to share experiences and exchange ideas to learn what works best.

I think we have put together a very interesting group of witnesses today. I look forward to their testimony, which I know will help us craft the best possible legislation to secure the government's vast and important treasury of information. Thank you very much.

Chairman THOMPSON. Thank you very much.

We are down to a minute or 2 on the vote, so we will recess for a few minutes to vote.

[Recess.]

Chairman THOMPSON. Let us go back into session.

Senator Akaka, did you have a statement.

OPENING STATEMENT OF SENATOR AKAKA

Senator AKAKA. Thank you very much, Mr. Chairman. Thank you for scheduling this hearing. I have a longer statement, Mr. Chairman. I will ask that my longer statement be made part of the record.

Chairman THOMPSON. It will be a part of the record.

Senator AKAKA. I just have a few points to make, three of them, to be exact. First, computer hacking has gone beyond the stage of being mischief making. Too much money is being lost. Hacking is a crime, but it has also become an act of international aggression. Last year, there were more than 20,000 cyber attacks on Defense Department networks alone.

Second, current technology has so far failed to provide adequate safeguards for critical infrastructure networks. We have little ability to detect or to recognize a cyber attack and even less capability to react.

Third, the President has unveiled his national plan for information systems protection. This, I feel, is a good proposal and deserves the immediate support of Congress.

Again, Mr. Chairman, my thanks to you. The legislation you have introduced on this subject, S. 1993, is something that we need to address immediately, and the Government Information Security Act is an important contribution. I look forward to today's discussion. Thank you, Mr. Chairman.

Chairman THOMPSON. Thank you very much.

[The prepared statement of Senator Akaka follows:]

PREPARED STATEMENT OF SENATOR AKAKA

Thank you, Mr. Chairman and Senator Lieberman, for providing the opportunity to discuss cybersecurity. In this new age of information warfare, no issue is of more vital importance to our security.

A cyber attack against our national information infrastructure would affect the integrity of our telecommunications, energy, banking and finances, transportation, water systems, and emergency services. As the Ranking Member of the Subcommittee on International Security, Proliferation, and Federal Services, I applaud all efforts to call attention to this issue. It is one in which the Subcommittee has also been involved. The Chairman and Ranking Member deserve great credit for the effort that they have made to heighten awareness of the threat while proposing methods to counter the threat.

Computer hacking can no longer be labeled benign mischief. Once, those who gained unauthorized access to government and private sector computer networks were heralded as technical icons, whose exploits were lionized by the popular media. That is not the reality any more. Now hacking is a Federal crime at the very least—at the worst, an international act of aggression. As Deputy Secretary of Defense John Hambre has stated, "We are at war—right now. We are in a cyber war."

Total losses from cyber fraud, including loss of service, recovery, and restoration costs, are estimated to be in the hundreds of millions of dollars. We now know that hostile countries have, or are developing, the capability to engage in overt and covert information warfare.

Last year alone there were more than 20,000 cyber attacks on Department of Defense networks alone. Astonishingly, we do not know who was behind the majority of those attacks.

In 1998, during a period of increased tensions with Iraq over United Nations weapons inspections, over 500 U.S. military, civilian government, and private sector computer systems were attacked. What was first thought to be a sophisticated Iraqi cyber attack proved to be a rather unsophisticated, yet highly effective attack by two juveniles from California with the cooperation of several individuals in Israel.

Last month, cyber-based denial of service attacks had a dramatic and immediate impact on many Americans and resulted in the loss of millions of dollars when several large e-commerce sites were shut down for several hours.

Just recently a student at a major university was arrested and charged with hacking into Federal Government computers at the National Aeronautics and Space Administration (NASA) and the Department of Defense where he was able to read, delete, and alter protected files and intercept and save log-in names.

Clearly, cybercrime has become a pervasive problem. And it is getting worse. According to FBI Director Louis Freeh, cybercrime is one of the fastest evolving areas of criminal behavior and a significant threat to our national and economic security. The escalation of cybercrime is rapidly overwhelming our current capability to respond.

Current technology has thus far failed to provide adequate safeguards for critical infrastructure networks. The Internet is international, knowing no boundaries and no ownership. Any attempt to stifle its growth and development would be counter productive to the economic interests of America. A variety of easy to use sophisticated hacker tools are freely available on the Internet, available for use by anyone in the world with an inclination to mount a cyber attack.

Today, the United States has little ability to detect or recognize a cyber attack against either government or private sector infrastructures and even less capability to react. Nevertheless, we must, through cooperative public and private sector efforts, develop adequate defensive technologies to neutralize threats. Without new defenses, it is likely that attacks will occur with greater frequency, do more damage, and be more difficult to detect and counter.

In January 2000, President Clinton unveiled his "National Plan for Information Systems Protection," which proposes critically needed infrastructure improvements with milestones for implementation. This multifaceted plan promotes an unprecedented level of public/private cooperation, and proposes 10 programs to assess vulnerabilities, and significantly enhance capabilities to deter, detect, and effectively respond to hacking incidents. It also calls for vital research and educational enhancements to train adequate numbers of desperately needed information security specialists and sustain their perishable skills.

Our continued leadership and prosperity in the global economy may well hinge on our national commitment to act as leaders in bringing information assurance to the global information environment we have helped to create. I commend the Chairman and Ranking Member for their leadership in calling attention to this particularly insidious problem by their introduction of S. 1993, the Government Information Security Act. I welcome our witnesses, and look forward to hearing their testimony today.

Chairman THOMPSON. Our first witness will be Kevin Mitnick. Mr. Mitnick, thank you for being with us here today. Please introduce yourself. Your full statement will be made a part of the record. If you could summarize that for us, we would appreciate it very much.

TESTIMONY OF KEVIN MITNICK[1]

Mr. MITNICK. Great. Good morning. It is an honor to be here. I am glad that you value my opinion. It is interesting to note that the United States was my adversary in years of litigation, and despite that fact, I am with you here today.

---

[1] The prepared statement of Mr. Mitnick appears in the Appendix on page 47.

Chairman THOMPSON. I have seen those documents several times, United States of America versus some individual. It is kind of intimidating, is it not?

Mr. MITNICK. It sure is. Despite that, I am ready, willing, and able to assist, and that is why I am here today. I have written a prepared statement. That way, I can just read it and hopefully will answer some questions.

Hon. Chairperson Thompson, distinguished Senators, and Members of the Committee, my name is Kevin Mitnick. I appear before you today to discuss your efforts to create legislation that will ensure the future security and reliability of information systems used by the Federal Government. As you know, I have submitted my written remarks to the Committee. I would like to use this time to emphasize some of those remarks and to introduce a few ideas that I did not include in my written testimony.

I have 20 years' experience circumventing information security measures and can report that I have successfully compromised all systems that I targeted for unauthorized access except one. I have 2 years' experience as a private investigator and my responsibilities included finding people and their money, primarily using social engineering techniques.

Breaching information security measures is a difficult undertaking. As I stated in my prepared remarks, my success depended on exploiting weaknesses in computer systems and network security and the use of social engineering techniques. However, even the sophisticated techniques I have exploited for 2 decades depended on the lack of commitment by software manufacturers to deliver software free of security weaknesses.

The manufacturers of operating systems and software applications are under enormous pressure to deliver their products to the market with new features and are unwilling to thoroughly test their software under current market conditions. As a result, operating systems and applications contain security flaws that allow people with the required time, money, resources, motivation, and persistence to exploit those weaknesses. The Federal Government has no control over the security weaknesses that software manufacturers permit to reach the marketplace. Thus, it is imperative to enhance other security measures to overcome these shortcomings.

The average American's confidence in the public telephone system is misplaced. Here is why. If I decided to target a computer system with a dial-in modem, my first step would be to use social engineering techniques to find the number of the modem. Next, I would gain access to the telephone switch that controls the number assigned to the modem line. Using that control, I would redirect the modem number to a log-in simulator that would enable me to capture the passwords necessary to access the target machine. This technique can be performed in real time to capture dynamic passwords that are changed once per minute.

All of the actions I just described would be invisible to anyone monitoring or auditing the target computer security. What is important here is to consider the big picture. People use insecure methods to verify security measures. The public's confidence in the telephone system as secure is misplaced, and the example I just described demonstrates the reason why.

The human side of computer security is easily exploited and constantly overlooked. Companies spend millions of dollars on firewalls, encryption, and secure access devices and it is money wasted because none of these measures address the weakest link in the security chain, the people who use, administer, operate, and account for computer systems that contain protected information.

It is my understanding that this Committee oversees information security for the Internal Revenue Service and the Social Security Administration. In the *United States v. Czubinski,* an IRS employee was convicted of wire and computer fraud, the same crimes for which I spent 5 years in Federal prison. It is not lost on me that Mr. Czubinski's conviction was overturned by the First Circuit Court of Appeals as the court found that he never deprived the IRS of their property interest in the confidential information he accessed just to satisfy his personal curiosity, the same circumstances which precisely match the crimes to which I plead guilty in March 1999.

Ironically, in their publicly filed briefs, the government revealed the name of the computer system used by IRS employees and the commands reportedly used by Mr. Czubinski and IRS employees in general to obtain confidential taxpayer information. I would like to bring to this Committee's attention how I successfully breached information security at the IRS and the Social Security Administration using social engineering techniques before 1992, which just so happens to be beyond the applicable statute of limitations. [Laughter.]

I called employees within these agencies and used social engineering to obtain the name of the target computer system and the commands used by agency employees to obtain protected taxpayer information. Once I was familiar with the agency's lingo, I was able to successfully social engineer other employees into issuing the commands required to obtain information for me using as a pretext the idea that I was a fellow employee having computer problems. I successfully exploited the security measures for which this Committee has oversight authority. I obtained confidential information in the same way government employees did and I did it all without even touching a computer.

Let me emphasize for the Committee the fact that these breaches of information security are ongoing and even as I stand before you today and that agency employees are being manipulated using social engineering exploits despite the current policies, procedures, guidelines, and standards already in place at these agencies.

S. 1993 is an important step toward protecting the confidentiality, integrity, and availability of critical data residing in government computer systems. However, after successfully exploiting similar security measures at the IRS and the Social Security Administration, as well as some of the planet's largest technology companies, including Motorola, Nokia, Sun Microsystems, and Novell, I am concerned that enacting this law without vigorous monitoring and auditing accompanied by extensive user education and training will fall short of the Committee's admirable goals.

In closing, I would be happy to offer my knowledge and expertise to the Committee regarding methods that may be used to counteract the weakest link in the security chain, the human element of information security. That is it. Thank you.

Chairman THOMPSON. Thank you very much. That was very short but very powerful, Mr. Mitnick. Thank you very much.

It seems, in essence, what you are telling us is that all of our systems are vulnerable, both government and private.

Mr. MITNICK. Absolutely.

Chairman THOMPSON. We had the members of The L0pft here a couple of years ago, some of the computer hackers, who basically told us the same thing. They said they could shut down the Internet and it was not a real problem. As I sit here and listen to you, you are one individual. Obviously, you are very bright, but there are a lot of very bright individuals out there. It makes you wonder, if one individual can do what you have done, what in the world could a foreign nation, with all the assets that they would have at their disposal do.

Mr. MITNICK. It is pretty scary.

Chairman THOMPSON. The point, and I think it is one that you make, is that we really do not know to what extent we already have been compromised, and the fact that we do not know or that other people or entities have not taken advantage of that or done something bad to us yet does not mean that we have not already been compromised in some way, is that not true?

Mr. MITNICK. It is a possibility.

Chairman THOMPSON. You also point out that the key to all of this, we sit here and think of systems and programs and all, but you point out the key is personnel, that that is the weakest link. No matter what kind of system you have, unless you have personnel that are adequately trained, adequately motivated—can you explain the importance of the personnel aspect to this and what you think we might be able to do about it?

Mr. MITNICK. In my experience, when I would try to get into these systems, the first line of attack would be what I call a social engineering attack, which really means trying to manipulate somebody over the phone through deception. I was so successful in that line of attack that I rarely had to go towards a technical attack. I believe that the government employees and people in the private sector, that their level of awareness has to be—you have to do something to raise their level of awareness that they could be the victim of some sort of scam over the telephone.

What I might suggest is maybe a videotape be made that would demonstrate somebody being manipulated over the phone and the types of pretexts and ruses that are used and maybe that will make somebody think the next time they get a phone call. The problem is, people do what they call information mining, is where you call several people within an organization and you basically ask questions that appear to be innocuous, but it is really intended to gain intelligence.

For instance, a vendor might call a company and ask them what software, what are you currently using, what computer systems do you have, to sell them a particular product, because they need to know that information, but the intent of the caller might be to gain intelligence to try to target their computer systems.

So I really have a firm belief that there has to be extensive training and education to educate the users and the people who administer and use these computer systems that they can be victims of manipulation over the telephone, because like I said in my prepared statement, companies could spend millions of dollars towards technological protections and that is money wasted if somebody could basically call somebody on the telephone and either convince them to do something on the computer which lowers the computer's defenses or reveals the information that they are seeking.

Chairman THOMPSON. So you can compromise a target without ever even using the computer?

Mr. MITNICK. Yes. For example, personally, with Motorola, I was working at a law firm in Denver and I left work that day and just on an impulse, I used my cellular telephone and called Motorola, their 800 number, and without getting into details of how this, because of the time constraints, is by the time I left work and by the time I walked home, which was about a 20-minute period, 15- to 20-minute period, without any planning or anything, I was able to, by the time I walked to the front door, I had the source code to the firmware which controlled the Motorola Ultralight telephone sitting on a server in Colorado. Just by simply making pretext telephone calls within that 15- to 20-minute period, I had the software. I convinced somebody at Motorola to send the software to a particular server.

Chairman THOMPSON. So this has to do with personnel, it has to do with training within a larger umbrella of management.

Mr. MITNICK. Absolutely, and I think the management has to be from top down, and the whole idea here is to protect the information regardless of whether it resides on a computer system or not, because whether or not this information is printed on a printout or is sitting on a floppy disk, it is still information which you want to protect against any type of confidentiality breach and the integrity of the information from being modified or destroyed.

Chairman THOMPSON. These are the things we are trying to address in our bill.

Mr. MITNICK. Yes, I read the bill.

Chairman THOMPSON. We appreciate your comments on that. One of the questions we are going to have to deal with is whether or not we ought to be more specific in terms of training, for example.

Mr. MITNICK. I think you should be, because——

Chairman THOMPSON. We vest the responsibility, but we kind of end it there and leave it up to the agencies to take it from there, but some have suggested that we might be more specific and more precise in exactly what kind of training we ought to have.

Mr. MITNICK. Yes, I think that is important because I am not privy to this information, but I assume that there are policies, procedures, guidelines, and standards in effect for protecting information at these agencies, just by protecting the information without regard to the computer systems. I think by explaining my background and experience with the Committee today that you can see that those policies and procedures were easily circumvented.

So what the Committee has to—I guess what has to be done is there has to be a way to figure out what the Federal Government could do to protect its information, and just enacting a law or policies and procedures may not be effective. I do not know. I think it really depends on really training the systems administration staff, management, and the people who use, administer, and have access to the information about all the different methodologies that could be used to breach computer security, which is not only just the human element. You have physical security, you have network security, and you have security of computer systems. So it is a very complex issue, so you have to be able to get people on board that would know how to protect each different area.

Chairman THOMPSON. We are not interested in another overlay of statutory requirements, and you are right, there are plenty of laws on the books that have to do with information systems in general. Technology has changed and the government has not changed with it, and what we have discovered is that although we have a lot of laws on the books, there is no comprehensive management scheme out there. There is no way to measure and evaluate the effectiveness of what anybody is doing. We will have a GAO witness here in a little while and we will go over the fact that for a few years now, we keep being told that government is ineffective. It is not working. It is not doing the job. So we go back and Congress does more. So that is what we are trying to do here and your testimony is very helpful.

We have other Senators here, so I will pass. Senator Lieberman.

Senator LIEBERMAN. Thanks, Mr. Chairman.

Mr. MITNICK. Can I make a comment?

Chairman THOMPSON. Yes.

Mr. MITNICK. And, by the way, private investigators and information brokers today obtain confidential taxpayer information from Social Security and the IRS and they are doing it as we speak. You can go to any private investigator and hire them to do this.

Chairman THOMPSON. We have had testimony to that effect.

Mr. MITNICK. So obviously it is somebody who has access to the computer either illegitimately or somebody that is taking payola to reveal this information that is within the agency.

Chairman THOMPSON. Thank you.

Senator LIEBERMAN. Thanks. Mr. Mitnick, thanks for your testimony. You have been very illuminating and helpful. My staff lifted up some clips in preparation and one of them described you as "arguably the most notorious computer hacker in the world." I thought I would ask you if you would be comfortable, as we confront this problem, helping us to answer the question of "why?"

I mean, in one sense, the "why" of a certain number of people, national certainly in security areas is clear. If a foreign government, such as the Serbs during the Kosovo conflict, or some subnational group of terrorists tries to break into our computer systems, that is a pretty clear "why."

But this is not like most crime waves. To a certain extent, as I read about your story and hear about others in the kind of daily breaking of government computer systems, it seems to me that there is a different sort of motivation. In some sense, it almost seems to be the challenge of it. If you would, just talk about why you, or if you want to third personalize it, why people generally become hackers.

Mr. MITNICK. Well, the definition of the word hacker, it has been widely distorted by the media, but why I engage in hacking activity, my hacking activity actually was—my motivation was the quest for knowledge, the intellectual challenge, the thrill, and also the escape from reality, kind of like somebody who chooses to gamble to block out things that they would rather not think about.

My hacking involved pretty much exploring computer systems and obtaining access to the source code of telecommunications systems and computer operating systems because what my goal was was to learn all I can about security vulnerabilities within these systems. My goal was not to cause any harm. It was not to profit in any way. I never made a red cent from doing this activity, and I acknowledge that breaking into computers is wrong and we all know that. I consider myself a trespasser and my motivation was more of—I felt like an explorer on these computer systems and I was trying—it was not really towards any end.

What I would do is I would try to obtain information on security vulnerabilities that would give me greater ability at accessing computers and accessing telecommunications systems, because ever since I was a young boy, I was fascinated with communications. I started with CB radio, ham radio, and eventually went into computers and I was just fascinated with it. And back then, when I was in school, computer hacking was encouraged. It was an encouraged activity.

Senator LIEBERMAN. Who encouraged it?

Mr. MITNICK. In school. In fact, I remember one of the projects my teacher gave me was writing a log-in simulator. A log-in simulator is a program to trick some unknowing user into providing their user name and password, and of course, I got an A—— [Laughter.]

But it was encouraged back then. We are talking about the 1970s. And now, it is taboo. A lot of people in the industry today, like Steven Jobs and Steven Wozniak, they started out by manipulating the phone system and I think even went to the point of selling blue boxes on Berkeley's campus, and they are well recognized as computer entrepreneurs. They were the founders of Apple Computer.

Senator LIEBERMAN. Yes. The fork in the road went in different directions in their case.

Mr. MITNICK. Just slightly. [Laughter.]

Senator LIEBERMAN. Well, maybe there is still time. You are young, so there is still time.

Your answer is very illuminating again. Part of what you are saying struck me, which is unlike other forms of trespass or crime, you did not profit at all.

Mr. MITNICK. I did not make a single dime, but that is not to say—one of the methods how I would try to avoid detection and being traced was to use illegitimate cellular phone numbers and electronic serial numbers to mask my location.

Senator LIEBERMAN. Right.

Mr. MITNICK. I did not use this to avoid the cost of making a phone call, because most of the phone calls were local. I could have picked up a phone at home and it would have been a flat rate call.

I did it to avoid detection, but at the same time, it was cellular phone fraud because I was using airtime without paying for it.

Senator LIEBERMAN. Were you aware as you went through this pattern of behavior that you were violating the law?

Mr. MITNICK. Oh, of course, yes.

Senator LIEBERMAN. You were? Were you encouraged or at least not deterred by the fact that you had some confidence that there were few or no consequences attached to it? There are cases where people know that they are doing something illegal, but they think that the prospects of being apprehended and charged are so slight that they go forward nonetheless.

Mr. MITNICK. Well, that is true, because as you are doing some illegal activity, you are not doing a cost-benefit analysis—well, at least I was not doing a cost-benefit analysis. I did not think of the consequences when I was engaging in this behavior. I just did it, but I was not thinking about, well, if I were to get caught, I would have these consequences. It was just focusing on the activity at hand and just doing it.

Senator LIEBERMAN. Because of what you described before as the thrill of it or the challenge of it, the adventure.

Mr. MITNICK. It was quest for knowledge, it was the thrill, and it was the intellectual challenge, and a lot of the companies I targeted to get the software was simply a trophy. I would copy the code, store it on a computer, and go right on to the next without even reading the code.

Senator LIEBERMAN. Interesting.

Mr. MITNICK. I mean, that is a complete different motivation of somebody who is really out for financial gain or a foreign country or a competitor trying to obtain information, like economic espionage, for instance.

Senator LIEBERMAN. Right, very different. Clearly, as a lawmaker, part of why I ask these questions is because I wonder whether if we raise the stakes, that is to say we set up security systems that make detection more likely and increase penalties for this kind of trespass, Internet trespass, whether there is a prospect of deterring the next Kevin Mitnick.

Mr. MITNICK. You are talking about enacting further criminal——

Senator LIEBERMAN. Yes, raising the prospects that a so-called hacker is going to be detected, for one, and then second, raising the criminal penalties for the hacking.

Mr. MITNICK. I would encourage you to come up with a method of prevention and detection, and I encourage the computer industry today to look to methods to better detect intrusions and, again, extensive user training and education on how to prevent the human exploitation.

For instance, in my case, I was basically doing this out of the curiosity rather than for financial gain, and what is interesting to note is in that case I described in that U.S. v. Czubinski case, where this was an IRS agent who obtained confidential taxpayer information and was eventually prosecuted, his convictions were reversed by the First Circuit Court of Appeals because what the court held is that Mr. Czubinski did not deprive the IRS of their property interest in this information because he had no intent to use or disclose the information he obtained.

That is the same circumstances as in my case. I was not doing it to use the information or disclose it to anybody. It was the trophy. So it is a very interesting issue of whether I really engaged in computer trespass or fraud, because fraud is where you deprive somebody of their money or property, and in my case, while it was a gross invasion of privacy, I never, in my opinion, deprived any of these companies of their software or used it to their detriment. So that is the difference in my hacking.

Then you have people out there who are working for private investigators, trying to obtain confidential information like from the IRS or Social Security and through State and local government agencies to sell. Information brokers sell it to private investigators who have clientele that are trying to find information on people.

Senator LIEBERMAN. You know, I hate to suggest a waste of your talent, but as I listen to you, I think you would make a great lawyer. [Laughter.]

Mr. MITNICK. Well, I do not know if you are convicted of a felony, if they would allow you to be admitted to the bar.

Senator LIEBERMAN. That is harder to do. [Laughter.]

Let me ask you just a few more questions.

Mr. MITNICK. Maybe I could get a Presidential pardon.

Senator LIEBERMAN. Yes. Maybe we will come back.

Chairman THOMPSON. We have a lot of criminal lawyers around here.

Senator LIEBERMAN. Yes, we do. [Laughter.]

Chairman THOMPSON. Nothing personal.

Senator LIEBERMAN. The response of the people attending was much more enthusiastic than we might like. [Laughter.]

Mr. Mitnick, building on what you have just said, obviously, you have been away, involuntarily, from the world of computers for a number of years now. I wonder if you feel that the techniques that you used are still useful today and whether they have retained their relevance in light of all the change that has occurred, and whether you have any sense that today's computer security systems are more sophisticated than they were when you were involved in your hacking.

Mr. MITNICK. Well, I can say that the social engineering or the exploiting the human element of computer security, I think is in the same state as it was 5 years ago before I went to prison.

Senator LIEBERMAN. Yes.

Mr. MITNICK. However, by reading materials and magazines and reading advertisements, I know that the industry is building security products to try to protect information that resides on computer systems. I have not had a chance to evaluate it, but it is simply if somebody has the resources, the time, money, and motivation, they can get into any computer. The only thing that the Federal Government and private sector can do is to reduce the threat. You cannot reduce it to zero——

Senator LIEBERMAN. Make it harder.

Mr. MITNICK [continuing]. You can only make it harder, and hopefully, the attacker will find it difficult that they will go to the next guy, just like people do at home. They put a lock on the door.

If somebody really wants to get in, they are going to go through a window, and you can only make it more difficult so they try to go to the next guy. Then if somebody is really targeted, government information or trying to target information in the private sector, I think it would be extremely difficult to prevent, and that is why management is so important to really encourage systems administrators and the users of these computer systems, maybe to do some sort of rewards program, or if information is breached under their control, there should be some punishment.

I have not really given it that much thought, but for the human element, I think it is still in the same state, and I believe there have been some technological improvements, but the Internet, do not forget, the Internet started out as the ARPANET, which was pretty much academia, government agencies, and universities sharing information and the protocols were not developed with security in mind. They were developed to allow these individuals or these companies to share information and to co-work on projects, and now everybody is scrambling because of the e-commerce to build security on top of a weak foundation. Maybe what should be considered is building a strong foundation.

Senator LIEBERMAN. Well said. I am struck by your emphasis on the human element as the weak link in this computer security chain and it conforms to other information we have heard that the so-called cultural factors, in some cases just plain negligence or inattention by people in charge of computers, leads to most of the problems in security that we have.

Let me ask one last question and then yield to my colleagues. In the question of security, as we think about computer security as it affects our national security, we naturally think of defense. But I have read some material that makes, I think, the good point that a hostile group or Nation wanting to do harm to the United States might not only go after traditional defense targets but might try to incapacitate power grids, for instance, public utility grids or transportation information systems or even stock or commodities markets.

To the best of your knowledge and experience, would you say that those essential but non-defense systems are probably as vulnerable as you have described systems to be generally?

Mr. MITNICK. Perhaps. If you have the resources of a foreign government, what would stop a foreign government from putting operatives to work in the companies to develop the hardware and software that is utilized by these groups, or the power grid, transportation, and these things of national importance, and put some type of back doors or some type of flaw in the operating system or the software applications that allows them to have access. I mean, they can go to those extremes and they have the resources to do it.

Senator LIEBERMAN. Your answer leads me to just ask one last question: You have talked about the prominent role of what you have described as social engineering, which is to manipulate unwitting employees. I know it is hard to state a percentage on this, but would you guess that most hacking is being done in that way-by the manipulation of the cultural weaknesses, the human weaknesses? And to that extent, how much does hacking depend on successful human penetration of a system as opposed to technological penetration of a system without any assistance from anybody inside, with the assistance from inside coming either knowledgeably, that is, by somebody who has been placed in there, or just unwittingly by a negligent employee?

Mr. MITNICK. In my experience, most of my hacking involved the social engineering exploitations, but I think that most of the hacking out there is really the weaknesses that are exploited in the operating systems and the software applications, because if you go on the Internet, you can simply connect to computer sites that basically have scripts of the exploit scripts, so anybody that has access to a computer and modem could download these exploits and exploit these vulnerabilities that are in the operating systems developed by the software manufacturers.

That is why I brought out the point that I think it is important for the software manufacturers to be committed to thoroughly testing their software to avoid these security flaws from being released to the marketplace.

Senator LIEBERMAN. It is a very important point.

Mr. MITNICK. And maybe government and private industry, if these companies are not committed to it, is maybe going with another company.

Senator LIEBERMAN. Thanks, Mr. Mitnick. You have been very helpful. I think you have turned your unfortunate experience in the past into some very constructive support this morning. Thank you.

Mr. MITNICK. Thank you for having me.

Chairman THOMPSON. How much time did you actually serve?

Mr. MITNICK. Fifty-nine months and 7 days.

Senator LIEBERMAN. Five years.

Chairman THOMPSON. Fifty-nine months?

Mr. MITNICK. I do not know how many minutes or hours.

Chairman THOMPSON. Well, you know if instead you had raised millions of dollars for political campaigns, you would have gotten probation. [Laughter.]

Senator Collins.

OPENING STATEMENT OF SENATOR COLLINS

Senator COLLINS. How can I follow that, Mr. Chairman?

Chairman THOMPSON. You had better choose your excitement more carefully in the future.

Mr. MITNICK. I think that is a good idea.

Senator COLLINS. Mr. Chairman, I want to first commend you and Senator Lieberman for holding this hearing to highlight the pervasive vulnerability of our private sector and government computer systems.

Mr. Mitnick, I was struck by your emphasis, as was Senator Lieberman, on the human element involved, because I think we often think of computer security in terms of technological safeguards or the physical security of the computers in restricting access. Yet your experience as well as the recent revelations about the former CIA Director's carelessness with his home computer suggest that we may be overlooking what is the most important factor, which is the human element.

In general, do you think there is a lack of awareness of the risks of the human element, both in the private sector and in the public sector? I am particularly thinking of at the higher levels of corporations and government agencies. I think training tends to occur at the lower levels, and yet the risk may be just as high at the higher levels. Could you comment on that?

Mr. MITNICK. I think the greater risk is at the lower levels. I do want to make a point. When you order a pizza, how they verify that you are the one that ordered it is by calling you on the telephone to verify that that is you. Well, you have got to really look at the big picture, and because there is a false reliance placed on telecommunications systems, such as the public telephone network, which is easily exploitable.

So, for instance, if I were to call you at your—what I did is offer to do a demonstration today if the government would give me immunity, but there was not any time. But anyway, what somebody could actually do is if they have access to the telephone switch, they could actually manipulate it so you can call back a legitimate number that you think you are calling to verify the authenticity of the request, but that number has been rerouted to the attacker. So because of the reliance on faxes, on voice mail, on telephones in general to verify the legitimacy, and that is easily exploitable, that is what makes it so easy to exploit the human element.

Senator COLLINS. How easy is it for a computer hacker to use work done by others—I am told it is called an attack script—in order to hack into a computer? Would such a person even have to really understand how the computer code was written in an attack script in order to use it to hack into a system?

Mr. MITNICK. Not really. If there is a shell script or a script is written where they just run it and it gives them the super-user privileges or system administrator privileges, they really do not have to know how it is working, and what is unfortunate, you have a lot of people out there that have access to those scripts that really do not know what they are doing, so if they get into a computer and obtain system administrator-level privileges, they could easily destroy information or damage the computer by trial and error and without realizing what they are doing because they do not have the knowledge or the experience on that particular type of computer system. So it is concerning.

Senator COLLINS. Another issue that you raised earlier was that when the Internet was in the early stages of development, the emphasis was on sharing information, accessibility, openness, free exchange of ideas. The emphasis was not on security and that has made us vulnerable in some ways.

Do you think that is also a problem with the growth of e-commerce, that there has been insufficient attention given to security, that the emphasis has been on accessibility, ease of use, making it easy for people to make purchases? Do you think the private sector has been a little bit slow in turning its attention and investing in the security of its systems?

Mr. MITNICK. Well, unfortunately, because I was unavailable for the last 5 years and e-commerce just started after I was sent away, I was not really able to keep up with it. But today, everybody is reluctant to use their credit card over the Internet because they think somebody is going to get their credit card number and defraud them. I think that there is a loss of confidence in using the Internet, especially with doing financial transactions, because mostly you hear about these media reports of these people being able to circumvent security so easily.

What is interesting is people will go into a restaurant and will hand their credit card number to a waiter or waitress and they have no problem with that, but they are afraid to type their number onto the Internet because they figure it could be captured, which is a possibility, but I think what is interesting is I think there is limited liability if someone were to obtain your card and use it without permission. There is maybe a $50 to $100 liability.

Maybe security systems have to be created that would raise the level of confidence that the public has in using the Internet for e-commerce.

Senator COLLINS. Thank you, Mr. Mitnick. I just want to wish you well as you go on with your life. You clearly have a great deal of talent and intelligence, and it seems to me, as we have been discussing, that you paid a pretty heavy price for your crime and I wish you well.

Mr. MITNICK. Thank you very much.

[The prepared statement of Senator Collins follows:]

PREPARED STATEMENT OF SENATOR COLLINS

Mr. Chairman, I appreciate the work you and Senator Lieberman have done on the important topic of the security of the computer system of the Federal Government.

The Internet offers unprecedented openness and accessibility. Those same attributes make it vulnerable to attacks by unauthorized users. The pervasive vulnerability of our computer systems raises the specter of malicious attacks by terrorists rather than simply the relatively benign intrusions of teenagers.

As one expert in computer security recently stated, "The Net changes the nature of crime. You don't need skills to be an attacker. If you are going to make counterfeit bills or burglarize a building, you need certain abilities. On the Net, you download an attack script and click here."

The sophistication of computers has been matched by the opportunity for malicious activity based on information obtained through the Internet. In my view, this creates an increased ability for a greater number of people to threaten government computers.

We have an excellent group of individuals on the panels today who can share their view of what the government can do to better protect its computer system. I look forward to their testimony.

Chairman THOMPSON. Thank you very much. Senator Edwards.

OPENING STATEMENT OF SENATOR EDWARDS

Senator EDWARDS. Thank you, Mr. Chairman.

Good morning, Mr. Mitnick.

Mr. MITNICK. Good morning.

Senator EDWARDS. I am from North Carolina and actually live in Raleigh and I remember vividly——

Mr. MITNICK. I have been there. [Laughter.]

Senator EDWARDS. You were big news for a long time in Raleigh. I remember it very well. Let me ask you about a couple of things. In answering one of Senator Lieberman's questions about why you got involved in hacking to begin with, I was listening to the words you were using and they sounded very much to me like a description of addictive behavior. Do you believe that addictive behavior is involved with folks who are habitually involved in hacking like you were?

Mr. MITNICK. I am not sure I would consider it addictive behavior. It was just an activity I was intensely interested and focused on, because ever since I was a young boy, I was interested in telecommunications and computers and that was just my calling, just like somebody is very interested in sports and every day they go out and practice. I am not sure that you can really equate it to like a physical addiction. But then again, I am not a health services professional, so I would not know.

Senator EDWARDS. No, I understand. But did you feel like you yourself were addicted to this hacking behavior?

Mr. MITNICK. I enjoyed it. I would say it was a distinct preoccupation, but I do not think I could label it as an addiction, per se.

Senator EDWARDS. Did you ever try to stop?

Mr. MITNICK. I did stop for a while, and then at that time that I was not engaging in that behavior, the Department of Justice, specifically the FBI, sent this informant to target me, and basically, I got hooked back into computer hacking because of the enticements that this fellow that they sent to target me, enticed me back into that arena.

Senator EDWARDS. What advice would you give to other hackers, or probably more importantly, potential hackers?

Mr. MITNICK. That is hard to say. I would have to really think about that. I do not encourage any activity which maliciously destroys, alters, or damages computer information. Breaking into computer systems is wrong. Nowadays, which was not possible for me when I was younger, computer systems are now more affordable and if somebody wants to hack, they can buy their own computer system and hack the operating system and learn the vulnerabilities on their own system without affecting anybody else with the potential for causing any type of harm.

So what I would suggest is if people are interested in the hacking aspect of computers, they can do it with their own systems and not intrude upon and violate other personal or corporations' privacy, or government.

Senator EDWARDS. Do you think it is possible to use things like click stream data to identify people who are least potentially going to——

Mr. MITNICK. Excuse me, to use what?

Senator EDWARDS. Click stream data. Do you know what that is?

Mr. MITNICK. No.

Senator EDWARDS. OK. Do you think there is some way to identify people who are likely to become engaged in hacking just based upon their patterns of behavior in using their computer systems?

Mr. MITNICK. I do not know.

Senator EDWARDS. You said in your testimony, and maybe someone has asked you this and I did not hear it, that in 20 years of experience in circumventing information security measures, you have been able to successfully compromise all systems save one.

Mr. MITNICK. That is true.

Senator EDWARDS. Which one?

Mr. MITNICK. It was a computer system run by an individual and this computer was at his home and it was in the U.K., in England, and I was unable to circumvent the security on that system because I did not have control of BT, which was British Telecom.

Senator EDWARDS. So there is nothing about the security system itself that gives us a lesson on how we can make systems more secure?

Mr. MITNICK. See, a real important point is the more people that have access to a computer system, the easier it is to penetrate because—well, of course, for the social engineering exploit, like in government or in large corporations, it is very easy. But the less people that have access to the computer system, the less vulnerable it is, and in this particular instance, it was one person and it was his home machine, so it was extremely difficult and this person was very, very sharp on computer security issues. In fact, this individual is the one that found security vulnerabilities in the VMS operating system which was manufactured by Digital Equipment Corporation, and why I targeted this individual was to basically find and obtain all the security flaws that he discovered in the operating system because my goal was obtaining information on all security vulnerabilities so I would be effective at being able to compromise any system that I chose to compromise.

Senator EDWARDS. One last thing. In North Carolina, we have a company called Red Hat.

Mr. MITNICK. Linux?

Senator EDWARDS. Yes. They have been, as you know, very successful. I had a meeting a few weeks ago with Bob Young, who is the founder of that company, and I was just curious whether you—and based on my discussions with him, I had some feeling that there was at least the potential for these open source software systems to be more secure. Do you have any views about that?

Mr. MITNICK. Yes. I think that is true, the reason being is they are open for inspection by the public at large and in so doing, just like with systems that utilize encryption, I think those security flaws could be readily identified and published and fixed rather than in a proprietary system where it is not open to the public and then you maybe have the individuals that find these holes do not report them and they use them to exploit vulnerabilities and access computer systems without anyone knowing the better, or without detection.

Senator EDWARDS. Thank you very much. Good luck to you.

Chairman THOMPSON. Thank you very much, Mr. Mitnick. You have been very, very helpful to us. Good luck to you.

Mr. MITNICK. Thank you.

Chairman THOMPSON. Thanks for being with us today.

Mr. MITNICK. It is an honor to be here today.

Chairman THOMPSON. I would like to introduce our second panel, Jack Brock, Director of Governmentwide and Defense Information Systems at GAO, who is responsible for most of the work done by the GAO for this Committee over the last few years. Also on the panel is Roberta Gross, the Inspector General for NASA, who has done much work in the area of computer security and even has a special investigative unit on computer crimes, so thank you for being with us.

We always take more time with our first panel, whether it is one witness or 10. We are going to have to be out of here in about an hour, so as far as we are concerned and the panels are concerned, let us keep that in mind and do what we can.

Mr. Brock, do you have any opening comments to make?

TESTIMONY OF JACK L. BROCK, JR.,[1] DIRECTOR, GOVERNMENTWIDE AND DEFENSE INFORMATION SYSTEMS, ACCOUNTING AND INFORMATION MANAGEMENT DIVISION, U.S. GENERAL ACCOUNTING OFFICE

Mr. BROCK. Yes, sir. I could actually spend my entire time reading you a list of the reports that we have done on computer security, many of these for your Committee.

Chairman THOMPSON. Could you summarize all that?

Mr. BROCK. Absolutely.

Chairman THOMPSON. Would you say there is a bunch?

Mr. BROCK. There are a lot.

Chairman THOMPSON. All right.

Mr. BROCK. Unlike Mr. Mitnick, when we go into agencies, we are doing so with the full knowledge and authorization of the agencies we go in. A long time ago, when we did computer security work, we examined agencies' controls and we would comment on those controls and we would say the controls are inadequate and the agency would say, well, no, they are adequate, so we disagree with you.

A few years ago, we started doing our own testing of the controls. We do not call it hacking, we call it penetration testing. We have been uniformly successful in getting into agencies. The reports that we have done for your Committee over the past few years at NASA, State, DOD, and the IRS, indicate that, typically, agencies have very poor controls.

EPA, which we have just released a report on a couple of weeks ago, we went in through their firewall, which offered virtually no protection. We had access to their mainframe computer center, which had almost no controls set up, and we were able to wander around the agency almost at will. It was not really difficult.

At another agency where the firewall offered better protection, we did what Mr. Mitnick was referring to as social engineering. We simply call people and say, I am Joe Blow. I am the system administrator. Here is my telephone number. Call me back. We are having a problem with your account. Give me your password, and you can call this number and check it. It is amazing how many people just call you right back and give you the password.

If that does not work, you just gain access to the building and walk around and you find computers that are open. You find the computer monitors with the password in a sticky on it. It is not very difficult to get access.

So as we have gone to agency after agency after agency, the specific weaknesses are usually technical. There is a technical reason that we are getting in. The software has a hole in it. The firewall is not very good. It is not very rigorous. Password protection is weak, or whatever.

[1] The prepared statement of Mr. Brock appears in the Appendix on page 55.

We, frankly, after doing many of these and we are doing the same report over and over, we said, there has got to be a better way of doing this, and at your request, we looked at agencies or at organizations that have good computer security, and there we found that good management attention to the problem is the secret. It is much like if you have a house and you have wood rot and people come in and they say, well, you have got a problem, and you patch it over with a little putty, you still have that underlying weakness.

We found when we were going into agencies and pointing out specific computer weaknesses, that these weaknesses would be corrected. They would patch it. But the underlying causes, the poor management, the lack of management attention, the lack of budget, all of these things really did not fix the underlying problem. So it was like sticking your finger in the dike. You would plug up one hole and another hole would spring out somewhere else and things would leak through. That is the condition we find at agencies, and we find it consistently.

One of the things that your bill does is it changes the direction of the computer security legislative framework. The Computer Security Act is inherently flawed in that it is built on a system-by-system basis. It starts with the premise that computer security can be fixed at the system level when really it needs to start at the management level. I would like to briefly go over a few features in your bill that we think are very commendable and we would encourage that if legislation is being considered, that these items be kept.

First of all, it incorporates the best practices that we found at leading organizations, in other words, those management practices that agencies or organizations undertook to, in fact, provide a secure framework throughout their organization.

Second, your bill requires a risk-based approach to be implemented by agency program managers and technical specialists. Let me just talk about this a little bit. If you do not know what your risk is, and risk is a function of the vulnerability of the system, a function of the threat to the system and a function of the value of the information of the process that that system controls. If you do not understand your risk, you are not going to put in the right kind of controls, you are not going to have the right kind of training, you are not going to have the right kind of testing. Rarely do we find agencies that do a good job at determining the risk they face, and again, without determining the risk, you are not going to know what sort of controls need to be put into place.

Third, your bill provides for an independent audit and we think that is an absolute must. An independent audit gives OMB, oversight committees, such as yourself, and agencies themselves an opportunity to see how well do controls work, how well do training policies work, how well are they doing as a management entity in terms of providing good computer security over our information resources.

Finally, it also eliminates the distinction between national security and non-national security systems. Right now, there is a dividing line. We have actually gone to some agencies and talked to them about computer security and they say, we do not have any classified information. Therefore, computer security is not an issue with us. And by having that distinction between national security and non-national security, we think that in many agencies, it creates a barrier to having an effective agency-wide security program.

If I could just indulge you for a moment more, we would like to talk about a couple of features that we think you should consider. The first of those, and you alluded to this in your opening remarks, is that we believe there should be mandatory standards put into place and that these standards should be in two parts. The first part would be a standard set of data classifications which would be used by all agencies, for example, risk levels ranging from one to whatever, and that data would be classified in one of these risk elements, ranging from things that you did not care that much about, information that was not particularly sensitive, was not particularly vulnerable, all the way to national security information.

In turn, this would lead to a set of mandatory control requirements that would set minimum requirements for each of these data classifications. We believe if this were instituted across the government, it would improve the ability of the government to enforce computer security, it would improve the ability of managers to provide a minimal level of support for their agency, it would permit better targeting of resources, and it would improve the ability of the independent auditors to do a good job.

Finally, we think there is also a need for stronger central guidance. I think the lessons learned from Y2K is that a strong central hand, in this case, John Koskinen, really can provide much needed oversight and impetus to agencies in terms of making sure that they are following good practices, making sure that budget submissions are responsive, and in general, providing the leadership that seems to be lacking in computer security.

That is my brief statement, and I would ask you, Mr. Chairman, that my full statement be included in the record.

Chairman THOMPSON. All statements will be made a part of the record. Thank you very much.

Chairman THOMPSON. Ms. Gross, thank you.

TESTIMONY OF ROBERTA L. GROSS,[1] INSPECTOR GENERAL, NATIONAL AERONAUTICS AND SPACE ADMINISTRATION

Ms. GROSS. Good morning. Thank you very much for inviting me here to testify on the act. I am here in a double capacity. I am here as the NASA Inspector General. I also head a task force that is looking at this bill on behalf of the Inspector Generals, and so I will weave in some remarks that will reflect some of the community remarks.

This is a world of limited budgets. We all know that. And in making decisions, agencies have to decide—Mr. Brock pointed that out—they have to figure out what is the risk to their systems. Obviously, in an agency like NASA, you are going to give a different kind of security to the public website than you would, for example, to protecting the astronauts on the space shuttle. So you have to make these risk/benefits and that requirement is a key element of this act.

[1] The prepared statement of Ms. Gross appears in the Appendix on page 71.

But there is a complication to agencies making investments in IT security. I think if you look at the Y2K issue, the problem of the change of the year for the computers, once it was a success, headlines were, this was maybe a hype and we spent too much money. Well, if it was not a success, there would have been a different set of headlines. So investment in IT security is very difficult for agencies to make, because if its security is working, you do not get headlines. But boy, when it does not work, you get headlines. I think recent events about the hackers attacking different systems, it makes headlines. But agencies do not see the visibility of IT security until it fails.

I would draw your attention to the success of the Y2K coordinated efforts. I think it provides a model that is reflected in your bill about how to approach IT security. It was at the highest level supported and everybody plugged in. You had the President, OMB, agency heads, the CIOs, GAO, and the IGs, as well as the Congress in its exercise of oversight, and the focus worked. We entered the new millennium with minimal Y2K problems.

This act asks many of the same players to have the same sustained focus, and that is key, a sustained focus. It was easy for Y2K, because it started rolling around and everybody started really focusing on it. But computer security is an ongoing effort, and I think it will be very helpful for this Committee and other committees with oversight to keep that sustained focus.

We (NASA OIG) support the placement of the focus of OMB, the Deputy Director, having oversight. I think it gives a high level attention. Also the Deputy Director has a unique vantage point. The Deputy Director serves as the chair for the IG councils, the CFO, the chief financial officer councils, the CIO councils, and also the president management councils (That is the very senior level executives that head up the agencies). And so you have a person at a high level that is able to coordinate all these different councils for a government-wide focus and I think that was a good selection.

You also make the heads of agencies to be accountable. Heads of agencies occupy bully pulpits. They are able to set the priorities of their agencies. Use the Y2K example. I can remember Dan Goldin saying, “I am being held accountable and we are not going to fail.” He had the bully pulpit and everybody heard. So this is enlisting again the heads of agencies, and you need to hold the agency heads accountable because they can change a culture of “I do not care,” or “we are just scientists,” or “we just want information, how does it impact me?” So that is a very important feature.

In terms of the CIOs, we had a discussion with the IG working groups. Many in the working groups view these CIOs as not having resources, not having staff, not having budget. Some even characterize their CIOs as paper tigers. So this act gives a lot of responsibility to the CIOs and it is going to be important for OMB and for this Committee and other committees to make sure that those CIOs have the authority and the resources to do what this act is expecting.

I would use the example of NASA. We have repeatedly made criticisms of the way that NASA establishes the CIO. He is doing the best he can, but he has no budget, or little budget, he has almost no staff, and NASA has decentralized the CIOs at each of the centers, and there are ten NASA centers. They (the center CIOs) do not report to him. He does not control their budget. He does not do their evaluation. The centers can give the CIOs collateral duties or they can decide what grade level the CIO should be: an SES, a 15, or a 14. If they do not agree, who do they report to? They report to the centers, not to the CIO, the head CIO. That decentralization and fragmentation impedes IT security.

To further compound that problem at NASA they have bifurcated, not bifurcated, they have given each of the centers various tasks. In Glenn in Ohio, the Glenn Center does training. In Ames in California, that is the center of excellence for IT security. You go to Marshall and that is the center for the firewalls, and on and on. Each center is a little center of excellence and none of those people report to the CIO. He does speak with them. They do collaborate. They do have telecons. But is it any wonder that it takes a long time for NASA to get any policies and procedures?

We have had reports pointing out instances where this decentralization and fragmentation, that whole kind of structure in and of itself weakens IT security, and we have more to say on that in my testimony, the written testimony.

I want to get to the part of the act that has to do with the Inspector Generals. In terms of the OIG working group, we did have a problem with the act narrowly defining the independent external auditor. Under the act, if the IGs do not do the work, an external auditor can be hired, but we thought that that implies a financial orientation and it should be any qualified external entity, and that is just a wording change.

But one of the things that the OIG working group commented on was they welcomed the act's tasking. They think you cannot be doing the high-risk work that agencies are facing without doing the review work, but the IGs will have to recruit, train, and retain a good cadre of professionals. That is going to require the support of the agencies and OMB and the Congress in supporting their budgets.

In my written testimony, I went through how for the past 4 years I have been recruiting a cadre of people in the audit arena and in the criminal investigative arena, as well as my inspectors, and that has taken time and these are a high-paid, qualified group. They are worth it. They are definitely worth it. But it does take time and it does take money and this group (Congress) has got to be supporting the budget that goes with that.

The last detail that I want to address is the section that talks about law enforcement authorities. The act requires that security incidents be reported to law enforcement officials, but it does not define that term. Where an OIG has a computer crimes division, then the agency system administrators need to report security incidents to and work closely with the IG special agents so that the agency ends up preserving evidence, maintaining chain of custody, and that you have the documents that you need and the materials that you need so that you can have a court case.

The Department of Justice has made clear in writings and in its actions that it is not just the FBI that does the criminal investigations on computer intrusions, and in my written testimony, I have a letter, referred to a letter by Scott Charney, who was then the former head of the Department of Justice Computer Crimes and Intellectual Property Division, where he talks about other agencies that do and have the authority for computer crimes—Secret Service, Air Force audit and their investigative service, as well as NASA's Inspector General. But I think that is very important for this oversight Committee to understand that.

Obviously, the Presidential Directive, PDD–63, established the NIPC, the National Infrastructure Protection Center, so that you can have the critical infrastructure reviews and investigations done by the FBI. But there are thousands of intrusions each year and every intrusion is not against the critical infrastructure. Indeed, at NASA, space does not even make the critical infrastructure. It is very important, then, that NASA have a good Inspector General's computer crimes unit, to have a group that has a focus on NASA as the victim.

It is important that this Congress support the efforts of Inspector Generals to have a computer crimes unit. It takes training. It takes training people. You have to have a very qualified cadre of people. But if you recall, the Inspector General Act was to have the synergism of audits and investigations so that if you are doing an investigation and you see internal control problems, you also tell your auditor so that they can do a system-wide look-see. That synergism is very important and it is very important that the Inspector General communities have computer crimes units so that the IGs can make sure that they protect the victim agencies.

In sum, I think you have the framework for a very good act. It has an oversight capacity, which I think is very important, and it also enlists the players that need to be there—OMB, heads of agencies, and CIOs. Thank you very much.

Chairman THOMPSON. Thank you very much. You were invited to come because of the innovative approaches that you have at NASA, and you remind us how important the IGs are in this whole process, so thank you very much for what you are doing and your helpful testimony.

Mr. Brock, let me address a few questions to you. The thing that jumps out at me first when I start to look at this, in February 1997, the GAO had a series of reports to Congress and things were so bad that this security problem was put on the high-risk list at that time. Late in that same year, 1997, the CIO Council, which is, of course, under the OMB, delineated it as a top priority. On March 31, 1998, the GAO filed another report on the consolidated financial statements and that report pointed out widespread deficiencies in terms of information security. Then again in September 1998, of course, we have this report entitled, "Serious Weaknesses Place Critical Federal Operations and Assets at Risk." I do not know how much more pointed you could be than that.

It is really outrageous that the Federal Government in an area of this sensitivity cannot do more faster. Since at least 1997, it has been 3 years since we have known—at least—since we have known about the seriousness of this problem. We get report after report after report. If I were you guys, I would wonder why you are even in business and whether or not we pay any attention to you or not. This last report still points out serious deficiencies, still do not have any management in the system, and we are still extremely vulnerable, and it makes you wonder what in the world it takes to get anybody's attention.

I look back at the current law and wonder, what are we doing to help the process? Are we overlaying an already complex process? I see we have given OMB responsibilities before. We have given agencies responsibilities before. Are we just telling them again to do it and we really mean it this time, or what are we really doing? I am playing devil's advocate with our own bill here, I guess, but are we really doing something here that is different from all of these other acts, the Computer Security Act, the Clinger-Cohen Act, Paperwork Reduction Act, on and on and on, the Privacy Act. I mean, you have a dozen pieces of legislation that in some way deal with this overall problem, so our solution is another piece of legislation. I am very skeptical, generally, of that problem.

Now, I do not want to waste my time or yours on this unless we are really doing something that, for the first time, can have some accountability. Until people are held accountable, until somebody is fired or somebody loses some money or somebody is embarrassed more than we have been able to so far, nothing is going to change. It looks to me like we have a chance here maybe of having some accountability. With the Results Act and everything, everybody is talking about measurements and measuring results and accountability from those results. I do not know whether we mean it or not yet, but we are all talking about it now, and now we are bringing it to this problem, measurable outputs and things like that.

First of all, is my assessment off base? If not, why has it taken so long to do anything and are we, in our bill, really doing anything that has a decent chance of making a difference?

Mr. BROCK. First, Mr. Chairman, as chairman of our oversight committee, I hope you were not really serious about wondering why we are in business. [Laughter.]

Chairman THOMPSON. Well, I would have to ask the same thing about ourselves, would I not?

Mr. BROCK. I agree with your basic premise. It is a shame that you have to have a bill to mandate good management. I mean, clearly, it is not a crime now to have good management in agencies that said, we are going to do things the right way. But clearly, the reports that we have done for your Committee over the past few years have indicated agencies are not doing the things the right way, that something is broken, and that attention needs to be paid to this.

I think the features you have in the bill, that many of these features are the kinds of things that are designed to pick things up by the nape of the neck and shake and grab attention. The independent assessments every year are a mechanism where you can identify weaknesses, where you can identify where accountability should lie and where it has not been exercised and where it gives the administration, as well as the Congress, an opportunity to take corrective action, and that is the next step. Pointing out the weaknesses, pointing out the management deficiencies is one thing, and then taking the next step to exercise that accountability is something that would still remain to be done.

Chairman THOMPSON. I take it that you feel that we need to be more specific in establishing standards.

Mr. BROCK. Yes, sir.

Chairman THOMPSON. Than the bill as currently drafted?

Mr. BROCK. Yes.

Chairman THOMPSON. And we need to delineate what with regard to risk levels, a requirement that they be considered or we tell them how to consider it, or how specific should we get on the mandatory requirements in determining risk level and also how specific in the mandatory minimum requirements, I guess you might say, in addressing those levels? Obviously, we cannot deal with all that here today, but——

Mr. BROCK. Your bill starts off in the right direction on that by requiring agencies to do a risk-based assessment. But once they do the assessment, they need to be able to categorize that. We have this level of risk, or we have this risk level. What category should that be in? How risky is it?

Chairman THOMPSON. That is really kind of management 101, is it not?

Mr. BROCK. Basically.

Chairman THOMPSON. I guess they do need to be told to do that.

Mr. BROCK. Basically, but if you had it consistent across the agencies, it would be much easier to have guidance that could be more easily developed and more easily taught and trained. But then the next step, if you are at a certain risk level, what are the minimum things you should do in terms of authentication, in terms of encryption, or in terms of independent testing to make sure that you are meeting those levels of control?

Chairman THOMPSON. So it would be a mistake to let each individual agency determine what it needed to do to address these because they have not shown any indication that they have the capability or the motivation to do that, is that correct?

Mr. BROCK. Yes. I think it is——

Chairman THOMPSON. You said it would be much easier to have minimum good standards that would apply to any agency.

Mr. BROCK. Right. I think it is appropriate for each agency to determine its risk that it faces, but then if you had the common standards. I think just the very process of developing those common standards would really create a rich dialogue and go a long ways towards improving a shared understanding among agencies about what some of the good features of computer security should be.

Chairman THOMPSON. And third, you mentioned some stronger central guidance. Obviously, OMB has not been doing its job. They have responsibility here. Now their major objection to your report, I understand, was that you are focusing too much on our responsibility at OMB and they either do not think they have that or want it. They are pointing to the agencies, and the agencies, I am sure, are pointing to somebody else. So here we go with OMB again, which causes some people to say we need a new information security czar, because maybe OMB inherently, if the allocation of their resources and what is going on over there, maybe they are not the right ones to be bird-dogging this. They sure have not done a good job of it so far.

What are we doing that is going to improve that situation? I understand that we cannot even tell where the money that we appropriate is supposed to go for, maybe it is not line item, but it is supposed to go for security enhancement. You cannot even find it. We do not know how it is being spent, in terms of information security, is that true?

Mr. BROCK. That is correct. We have trouble determining how much money is spent within each agency on computer security. I think Ms. Gross in her statement, when she talked about the similarities between the Y2K problem and how top managers within each agency felt accountable, and I think one of the reasons they felt accountable was really the strong role that the central manager, in this case, Mr. Koskinen, made in making sure they understood they were being held accountable.

We do not have that situation on computer security. I think it should be closely examined as to whether there should be a computer security czar, though, and separate that from a CIO that would have responsibilities for other aspects for information management. We have rarely gone to a good organization that had good computer security, and we found out when we go there that they also have other good information management practices. It is part and parcel. We have never gone to a place that had poor information management, where they had poor lifecycle management, poor systems development efforts, poor software acquisition processes and had good computer security. It all runs together.

Therefore, I would be reluctant to suggest that you separate computer security from the other aspects of information management. Next year, the OIRA reauthorization will be coming up and you will have an opportunity at that time, as well, to examine the Paperwork Reduction Act, the Clinger-Cohen Act, as well, and I think these are good questions to also bring up at that time.

Chairman THOMPSON. We are looking forward to that, but we are not vesting responsibility there in this bill. We are bringing it to a little higher level than that, but thank you very much.

Senator Lieberman.

Senator LIEBERMAN. Thanks, Mr. Chairman. Thanks to both of you. I think your testimony, both written and here today, has been really very direct and very helpful and you are both obviously quite knowledgeable. The Chairman has covered some of the areas I had an interest in, so I will be fairly brief.

I take it that you agree not only with what Mr. Mitnick said, but what I have learned generally in my reading here, that a lot of the problems of computer security are cultural, which is to say human, correct?

Mr. BROCK. Yes.

Senator LIEBERMAN. Beyond management, which obviously is critical and at the heart of this, let me just ask you to speak a little bit more about the question of whether there should be consequences if a Federal employee fails to follow proper procedures relating to computer security. Or, on the other end, whether there ought to be consequences for exemplary behavior with regard to computer security.

Mr. BROCK. Yes, I would agree with that. The problem we have, though, and some Federal agencies are going to, that accountability is always at the technical level. Well, we have had a break-in, we have had a failure, it must be the guys in the computer room's

63-639 00 - 2

fault or we would not have had this. And for specific weaknesses, that might well be true, but the accountability typically does not extend upwards into management, where an atmosphere has been created or budget resources have not been appropriated or whatever and those individuals also need to assume their share of the accountability.

In the private sector, we found very definite links and control mechanisms for measuring accountability, for measuring performance against that accountability and holding individuals responsible, whether they be system administrators or the system process owners.

Senator LIEBERMAN. How are they held responsible in the private sector?

Mr. BROCK. In one good example we have, managers have to define the risk. Along with the technical people, they agree upon the vulnerabilities and the threats. They then have to allocate money and resources to providing an appropriate level of protection and they sign off on that. At the end of the year, the independent audit comes in and, first of all, determines did you, in fact, appropriately determine the risk and are you appropriately protecting these to the level you agreed upon.

In some cases, we found good examples where they made a business decision not to provide a level of protection, but it was a business decision and it was examined and agreed upon by the board. And in some cases, I believe that people were fired when they failed to meet the terms of their contract.

Senator LIEBERMAN. Ms. Gross, do you want to add anything about individual accountability here?

Ms. GROSS. Yes. I think what you have to do is first implement a training program——

Senator LIEBERMAN. Right.

Ms. GROSS [continuing]. Because this is very much a cultural thing. I mean, NASA, you go to, for example, the Goddard Space Center and its scientists, its engineers, they are collegial. They are talking with universities and they are interested in their earth science programs and they do not think about security. It is not until, for example, you will tell a scientist who is collecting data and working on a journal article, if somebody takes your information through the computer and publishes that information a year ahead of you or 6 months ahead of you, do you care? Oh, they all of a sudden—it comes home that it actually does impact them.

Senator LIEBERMAN. Sure.

Ms. GROSS. And I think the GAO audit on NASA pointed out they did not have a training program. They still do not. They are still getting it together and trying to work out what should be the appropriate training program, partially because they did not have IT security standards, so how can you develop your training program. But meanwhile, you have to have systems administrators trained. They expect to have it in 2001. You cannot wait until 2001. You have got to have systems administrators held accountable in some ways.

So the issue on accountability is a lot more complex than just saying, you have got to be accountable and we are going to take action. On the other hand, on very simple, no-cost, low-cost things that the agency can do, they should be held accountable. They are supposed to banner their systems, both for law enforcement and for downstream liability, it is supposed to say, this is a government computer, you are accessing a government computer, so the hacker knows he is trespassing. He cannot say, oh, I was just surfing. I was looking for America On-Line and look what I got, I got NASA.

So bannering is simple, but it does not happen. In that case, if a system administrator is not going to banner the computer, we just take away the computer. They cannot do their science. That you can hold for simple, no-cost, low-cost, which we have identified and we can continue to identify. You can hold them accountable because it makes the agency safer right away.

On the other hand for some of the major accountabilities, you have to have risk assessments and you also have to then make sure that your systems administrators, and that is not insignificant numbers, are trained, and let me explain why I am saying it is not an insignificant number.

For example, the Goddard Space Center, they said, how many of you think that you are system administrators, in other words, you have basically root access and have super controls of the computer. Nine hundred people need a basic training and an advanced training so that they can be systems administrators, and in many of those cases it is a collateral duty. They are not security specialists, they are scientists, but they have a very powerful computer system that networks with other systems, so they need training.

So I am trying to put it in a context, because you can say, OK, we are going to hold people accountable and we should have very powerful consequences. I think that, definitely, agencies can start immediately, no cost, low cost. There is no reason why agencies cannot be bannering their computers. That is nothing new.

Senator LIEBERMAN. Right.

Ms. GROSS. There is no reason why people cannot be using passwords that are a little more difficult than the dictionary. I mean, the security office gives instructions on how to have better passwords. All those things, you can start holding people accountable for, and I think what you end up having to have is your CIO making a range of things that we expect tomorrow or next week, and these are the other things we are going to phase in, but it takes attention, and again, you start with the bully pulpit of the head of the agency. You (Congress) all have the bully pulpit also, and that is important, but the agency does, too.

Senator LIEBERMAN. Right. I think the intention of the bill—though it does more than this—is to raise up computer security as a priority consideration of Federal agencies and of individual Federal employees who have responsibility.

Let me ask a last question of you, Mr. Brock. I am sure you know that the President proposed a Federal Intrusion Detection Network, FIDNet, to monitor patterns of intrusions in the Federal systems, which is supposed to be housed at GSA's Federal Computer Incident Response Capability office.

Mr. BROCK. Yes.

Senator LIEBERMAN. In your testimony, you mentioned the need to improve the government's ability to respond to attacks on computer systems. So my question is, just to build a bit on whether we need a stronger Central Incident Response Center, whether the President's idea and location is the right one.

Mr. BROCK. Well, those all go together.

Senator LIEBERMAN. Right.

Mr. BROCK. We do believe that incident response is important and that intrusion detection is important. A specific criticism we had of the President's plan was the fact that it focused so much on intrusion detection, you began to get the impression that that was the primary means they had of improving the government's or the Federal Government's computer security program.

Senator LIEBERMAN. You mean as opposed to all the other management——

Mr. BROCK. As opposed to prevention, for example.

Senator LIEBERMAN. Prevention, right.

Mr. BROCK. One agency that we have gone to at EPA, they did a pretty good job of reporting and recording their intrusions. They did a very bad job of doing anything to prevent those intrusions or in analyzing those intrusions in order to take corrective action.

So intrusion detection is important. It is important to share that information with other agencies so that you can learn from it. So to that point, we strongly support sharing the information. We would strongly support some sort of incident response capability so that you could take action, but it needs to be part and parcel of an entire program and should not be the primary or the only focus of such a program.

Senator LIEBERMAN. Thanks very much. Thank you both. That was very helpful.

Chairman THOMPSON. Thank you very much. We could spend a lot of time with the both of you. You have been very helpful today and we will continue to work together on this. We appreciate your contribution to this and your fine work.

Mr. BROCK. Thank you.

Ms. GROSS. Before I go, I would like to just incorporate into the record my full written testimony.

Chairman THOMPSON. Absolutely. All statements will be made a part of the record.

Ms. GROSS. And both Senators, I would like to leave for you all, we have done a "Clearing Information From Your Computer's Hard Drive" pamphlet. Mr. Mitnick was saying how easy it is at the lowest levels to end up having intrusions. This is when you excess your computer and you get a nice new super computer and you think you have deleted all your files and what happens is a lot of your information that you think is very sensitive is going out to schools, to prisons, etc. We have some on the desk and I certainly draw this to your attention. Thank you.

Chairman THOMPSON. Thank you very much.

On our third panel, we are fortunate to have Ken Watson, Manager of Critical Infrastructure Protection at Cisco Systems, Inc., and James Adams, who is the CEO and co-founder of iDEFENSE. Both of these gentlemen are known in the industry as experts on the issues related to information protection and security.

Gentlemen, thank you very much for being with us here today. Mr. Watson, do you have an opening statement to make?

TESTIMONY OF KENNETH WATSON,[1] MANAGER, CRITICAL INFRASTRUCTURE PROTECTION, CISCO SYSTEMS, INC.

Mr. WATSON. Thank you, Chairman Thompson, Ranking Member Lieberman, and distinguished Members who are here. I appreciate the opportunity to speak to you about network security best practices.

The last 8 years of my 23 years in the Marine Corps I spent helping to draft policy and doctrine for information warfare and taking joint teams and conducting information operations to integrate those into other military operations. When I retired, I went to work for WheelGroup Corporation, where I managed our security consulting team. We would do legal contracted security posture assessments in corporate networks and provide them reports of their vulnerabilities. When Cisco acquired WheelGroup, I transitioned to critical infrastructure protection and that is my role now at Cisco.

That team just recently conducted a 6-month study of vulnerabilities in corporate networks and I have put together the top three to five vulnerabilities that were discovered in every area as the last two pages of my written testimony and it is just a table of what are the vulnerabilities and how do you fix them. It is important to note that the way this team works, it does not use anything like social engineering or other things that might cross the bounds into becoming illegal activities. They concentrate on working at the keyboard only and finding technical vulnerabilities and that is it.

It is kind of interesting that they are continually successful in penetrating external defenses about 75 percent of the time, but once inside, they are about 100 percent successful in gaining unauthorized access between machines inside a network, and that would be true for government or private sector networks.

Cisco systems is serious about network security and about its implications for critical infrastructures on which this and other developed nations depend. Few can argue that the Internet is changing every aspect of our lives. Internet economy is creating a level playing field for companies, countries, and individuals around the world. In the 21st Century, the big will no longer outperform the small. Rather, the fast will beat the slow.

So how do you decide on a best practices solution? I would like to offer a simple way to organize network security technologies and practices and talk a little bit about what Cisco has seen in customer networks. Our model is not reinventing the wheel, but it is what we call the security wheel and it talks to five general areas where you can group technologies and practices and it is a management model.

Good security must be based on policy. Employees must know what they can and cannot do with company systems or government systems and that they will be held accountable by whoever is the boss, the CIO or whoever is accountable, and those people should be accountable, also.

The policy must also be risk-based, so I am in concurrence with a lot of what you have already heard today.

---

[1] The prepared statement of Mr. Watson appears in the Appendix on page 83.

After setting appropriate policies, a company or organization must methodically consider security as a part, an integrated part of normal network operations. This could be as simple as configuring routers to not accept unauthorized addresses or services, or as complex as installing firewalls, intrusion detection systems, authentication, and encrypted virtual private networks.

A basic tenet of military combat engineers is that an unobserved obstacle will eventually be breached, and that is also true for networks. Hackers will eventually figure a way around or through static defenses. The number and frequency of computer attacks is constantly on the rise. There are no vacation periods. As such a critical part of the security wheel is to monitor the network, intrusion detection and other monitoring devices, so that you have 24 by 7 visibility into what is going on inside and outside the network.

The next stop is testing the network. Organizations that scan their networks regularly, updating electronic network maps, determining what hosts and services are running, and cataloging vulnerabilities, and they should also bring in experts for independent network security posture audits once or twice a year to provide a more thorough assessment of vulnerability.

It is just like cleaning your teeth. We brush our teeth every day. Those are like your internal own network scans. And you go to the dentist once or twice a year and get an independent outside observation. It may be painful, but you get a lot of good out of it in the long run.

Finally, there needs to be a feedback loop in every best practice. System administrators must be empowered to make improvements. Senior management has to be held accountable for network security. Those involved in day-to-day operations must have their attention.

If you were to ask me, what is the most important step to do right now, I would give you two answers, one for the short-term and one for the long-term. In the short-term, the best thing I think any company or organization can do is to conduct a security posture assessment along with a risk assessment to establish a baseline. Without measuring where you are, you cannot possibly figure out where you need to go.

For the long term, the best thing we can do together is to close the alarming skills gap. The requirement for highly skilled security specialists is increasing faster than all the training programs combined can produce qualified candidates. Universities are having difficulty attracting both professors and students. The government is also having a hard time retaining skilled security professionals. We in the private sector are building and maintaining state-of-the-art security training programs and we are collaborating with education institutions and training partners to provide a wide base for delivery.

We are also helping the Office of Personnel Management to identify knowledge skills, abilities, and ongoing training requirements and career management and mentoring ideas for a Federal IT security workforce. This human resources issue is by far the most critical information security problem we face in the long term and the solution must be based on government, industry, and academic collaboration.

Corporate network perimeters are blurring. That is also true for the lines between government and industry. The Internet knows no boundaries and we are all in this together. We are very enthusiastic about the new Partnership for Critical Infrastructure Security, a voluntary organization of some 120 companies from across the country dedicated to improving the network security of our critical infrastructures.

As we further build the relationship between the public and private sectors, we hope the great spirit of cooperation currently led by the Department of Commerce and the Critical Infrastructure Assurance Office will continue.

We believe that confidence in e-commerce is increasing. Thirty-eight new web pages are being added to the World Wide Web every second. Our job, all of us, all of our job, is to raise the bar of security overall, worldwide, so that we can empower our citizens and customers to take full advantage of the Internet economy in the Internet century.

Thank you very much. I will be glad to answer any questions.

Chairman THOMPSON. Thank you very much. Mr. Adams.

TESTIMONY OF JAMES ADAMS,[1] CHIEF EXECUTIVE OFFICER, INFRASTRUCTURE DEFENSE, INC.

Mr. ADAMS. Chairman Thompson, Ranking Member Lieberman, thank you very much for including me on this distinguished panel.

By way of brief background, my company, iDEFENSE, provides intelligence-driven products—daily reports, consulting, and certification—that allow clients to mitigate or avoid computer network information and Internet asset attacks before they occur. As an example, iDEFENSE began warning its clients about the possibility of distributed denial of service attacks, the kind of hacker activity that is capturing headlines currently around the world, back in October and November of last year.

At the outset, I would like to commend you and your staff for crafting such thoughtful and badly needed legislation in the area of computer security for the Federal Government. We are currently in the midst of a revolution, the information revolution, which calls for dramatic and bold steps in the area of securing cyberspace. It is in this context that your bill takes a crucial step forward by shaking out the current culture of lethargy and inertia gripping the Federal Government. With a proposal to put teeth into the OMB's oversight of computer security issues, this bill is a solid step in the right direction.

Why does this matter? Few revolutions are accomplished without bloodshed. Already, as we plunge headlong and terribly ill-prepared into the knowledge age, we are beginning to receive the initial casualty reports from the front line of the technology revolution and to witness firsthand the cyber threats that, if allowed to fully mature, could cause horrendous damage.

The recent denial of service attacks were mere pinpricks on the body of e-commerce. Consider instead that some 30 countries have aggressive offensive information warfare programs and all of them have America firmly in their sights. Consider, too, that if you buy

[1] The prepared statement of Mr. Adams appears in the Appendix on page 88.

a piece of hardware or software from several countries, among them some of our allies, there is real concern that you will be buying doctored equipment that will siphon copies of all material that passes across that hardware or software back to the country of manufacture.

The hacker today is not just the stereotypical computer geek with a grudge against the world. The hacker today is much more likely to be in the employ of a government or big business or organized crime, and the hackers of tomorrow will be all of that and the disenfranchised of the 21st Century who will resort to the virtual space to commit acts of terrorism far more effective than anything we have seen in the 20th Century.

The government, in all its stateliness, continues to move forward as if the revolution is not happening. Seven months ago, my company won a major contract with a government agency to deliver urgently needed intelligence. The money was allocated, the paperwork done. Yet, it remains mired in the bureaucratic hell from which apparently it cannot be extricated. [Laughter.]

Another government agency is trying to revolutionize its procurement processes to keep up with the pace of the revolution. They are proudly talking about reducing procurement times down to under 2 years. In other words, by the time new equipment is in place, the revolution has already moved on 8 Internet years. In my company, if I cannot have a revolutionary new system in place within 90 days, I do not want it.

The Thompson-Lieberman legislation is a good first step to try and control and drive the process that will bring the government up to speed with this revolution. I believe, however, that to effectively cope with the technology revolution, this proposal must be strengthened. What is needed is an outside entity with real power to implement drastic change in the way government approaches technology and the underlying security of its systems. Currently, jurisdictional wrangling, procurement problems, and a slew of other issues are seriously hampering the government's ability to stay current.

The Thompson-Lieberman bill provides a framework to begin sorting through this mess. However, what is needed most is a person or an entity that will draw on skill sets in many areas that will overlap that of the CIOs, CFOs, CSO, and most of the other officers or entities that currently exist. Let us give this person the title of Chief of Business Assurance, or perhaps the Office of Business Assurance, to relate it directly to the Federal Government.

The OBA's task would be to continuously gather and synthesize infrastructure-related trends and events, to intelligently evaluate the technological context within which the organization operates, to identify and assess potential threats, and then to suggest defensive action, or viewed from the positive side, to assess the technological revolution's opportunities and propose effective offensive strategies. The OBA must be a totally independent organization with real teeth and real power.

There is much in common between government and industry when it comes to the challenges and the opportunities that the technology revolution poses. Both sectors face a common threat. Both factors share common goals for the well-being of America and her people. Both employ technologies that are, in essence, identical, and both must work together to protect each other.

I leave you with this thought. In the near term, you will see total transformations of the way business and government is conducted, internally and externally. A failure to change to meet these new challenges is to risk the destruction that all revolutions bring in their wake. Proactive action is the route to survival.

We have heard a great deal in recent months about the potential of a digital divide developing between the computer haves and the computer have-nots. I believe there is another digital divide that is growing between the American Government and its citizens. If this Committee's efforts do not move forward in changing this culture of inertia, there is real danger that the digital divide that exists between government and the private sector will only widen. We cannot afford a situation where the governed feel that their government is out of touch and increasingly irrelevant to their lives. By stepping up to the plate and tackling computer security with an innovative, bold approach, the Thompson-Lieberman bill significantly boosts the chances of reversing the current bureaucratic approach to a very dynamic problem.

Thank you again for the honor of appearing before you.

Chairman THOMPSON. Thank you, Mr. Adams. Very well said.

You heard me mention, I am sure, a while ago about all of the reports and assessments and so forth over the last 2 or 3 years pointing this out. Now, in addition to all of that, we have the President's first version of the National Plan for Information Systems Protection. The plan discusses the need to make the government a model for cyber protection.

As I look at it, I see few concrete proposals as to how to do that. As you know, I am mindful of these overlays and these impressions that we try to leave sometimes that we are doing something when we are really not. Where does this plan fit into the solution to what we are talking about here today?

Mr. ADAMS. Well, I would just say a couple things about that. First, the plan was 7 months late. It is not a plan, it is an invitation to dialogue, a very different thing. If you asked those who were involved in the formulation of the plan, they will tell you that it was a "business as usual, government at work" nightmare. Every meeting, 100 people would turn up. They would talk about not what was good for the Nation but what was good for their existing equities.

The result was a bureaucratic compromise, which is the document that you see, that raises some interesting points. But a plan will actually emerge, I would guess, a year from now, longer. Meanwhile, we all march on. It requires, I think, more than that, and where the action will have to come from and the leadership will come from is exactly right here. It is not going to come from the Federal Government as we know it, because it is a revolution and governments do not become revolutionaries. They naturally evolve, which is a great strength in a democracy. But in the middle of a revolution, it is actually a threat and a challenge to us that we need to step up to try and meet.

Chairman THOMPSON. So we are trying to do something very tough but very necessary, is what you are saying.

Mr. ADAMS. Absolutely, and the great thing, I think, that you are doing is saying, yes, this needs to be done. The very difficult thing for you, as you were rightly articulating earlier, is how to force what needs to be done to actually occur, because you say to the OMB, an inert bureaucracy in its own right, you have to force other organizations to change. True, but how exactly, and typically, it does not work like that.

If you look at what the CIA is doing to try and embrace the revolution, they formed an outside organization, INCUTEL, that is driving technology revolution into the organization and pushing change from without to within, and to expect or ask organizations that are comfortable with business as usual to say, no, no, no, revolutionize, they will not do it. Imposition of change is the only way it will occur, and it will be resisted, but the consequence of not doing it can be very, very serious, and you can already see how relevant does anybody in Silicon Valley think the government is—not at all.

Mr. WATSON. If I might add a comment——

Chairman THOMPSON. Yes, go ahead.

Mr. WATSON. Mr. Chairman, the plan is not a complete plan yet, but at least——

Chairman THOMPSON. We are relevant in terms of the harm we can do them and how we can mess things up. From a positive standpoint, it is a very good question. Excuse me. Go ahead.

Mr. WATSON. But at least there was enough foresight in the Critical Infrastructure Assurance Office to at least get a plan started, and it is an invitation to a dialogue. They have asked industry to help complete this plan, add our perspective, bring in a physical dimension, look at the international aspects that are not in the current plan. I look forward to working with the Partnership, the big "P" Partnership that we just launched, to help make that come to pass.

Chairman THOMPSON. It has taken 3 years since this all has been on the high-risk list, and now, when we cannot even take a baby step, we are talking about flying an airplane, and international and all these other high-sounding things which may eventually come about when China becomes a full democracy.

Let me explore, you obviously feel like we have to have some kind of an outside entity. You refer to the OBA. Where does this individual fit into the process? What kind of entity are you talking about? Who is this person? How is this person selected? Who are they accountable to? I take it it is not within OMB, is what you have got in mind. Have you thought that through to that extent?

Mr. ADAMS. I think OMB has got a long and traditional role in oversight and it does that job and has done so for a long time. It would be possible to have something sitting outside of OMB but working within the Federal Government structure but with a rather different mandate.

If you look at the way industry sets up revolutionary change, it does so by—Steve Jobs and Apple is a good example. Put them in a different building, you set them outside the culture, you put a pirate flag on the roof, they develop their own language and culture and they come up with new and creative ideas.

What we see at the moment is the traditional organization says we will go to the traditional places, the traditional consulting companies. They are use to forming committees, punching button A, producing a report in 6 months. Everybody thinks about it and does not do anything. Meanwhile, the people who really are making this revolution occur are the very different organizations that are the dot-com companies, and there needs to be some mechanism for allowing them to have input into change.

So I would envisage something where you, Congress, would mandate and budget a group that would have the ability and the authority to impose change. Now, there is a thought, to impose, and if you do not do it, you will be held accountable in a culture, remember, where many of the things that government has traditionally thought of as its own self.

To take Cisco, for example, they have 26,000 employees. They have three people in the whole organization doing expense accounting. Now, in the government, you have hundreds and thousands or however many people doing the process that can be outsourced. So we need to think about this and how can we make government efficient, relevant, fast moving, changing, dynamic, and I do not believe that it can be done imposing internal solutions.

Processes and all of those things need to come from outside—technology, people, and processes. They will not be able to meet the technology because they cannot procure it fast enough. They cannot hire the people because they cannot afford them. We cannot, and we are paying much more money. And you will not have the processes because you need to impose them in a constantly dynamic way. So those three things will have to come from outside, and the only place that can mandate it, I think, is Congress, which will enforce it, enforce a different structure, a different way of thinking.

Chairman THOMPSON. Thank you. Senator Lieberman.

Senator LIEBERMAN. Thanks. Again, thanks to both of you. I think, Mr. Chairman, we have had really excellent witnesses today.

Mr. Mitnick earlier made the allegation that part of the problem here, though, as you know, he focused on the human management problem, is that there is such competition, particularly among software manufacturers, to get the product out to the market quickly that they are not spending sufficient time to deal with potential security flaws in that software. In fact, you have actually gone one step to the other side, really stunningly, or to me, fascinatingly, in saying that some foreign manufacturers may, in fact, be putting, I do not know whether you would call it a virus or something in the system that allows it to divert information back to them to be more easily hacked.

Let me ask you to go at both parts of that. First, whether Mitnick has a point that manufacturers are not spending sufficient time dealing with systems to stop security problems before they put their products on the market.

Mr. ADAMS. Well, we clearly know that that is correct. The rush to market, speed is of the essence. You clearly do not waste time. They are able to get away with that partly because we are all rushing forward with the revolution and absorbing it as fast as we can, and partly because there is not any training, there is not any process, and people are not security aware.

If there was, as Jack Brock was talking about earlier, a minimum benchmark above which you have to be, then there would become a market-driven demand. I am not going to buy this software because it just simply does not meet my minimum standard, but I will buy this because it does. So there will be a market-driven enforcer that would say, if you do not raise your standards to become more security aware, you are out of business.

Senator LIEBERMAN. Yes. In other words, people who are doing it may advertise that as an attribute, for instance——

Mr. ADAMS. Absolutely.

Senator LIEBERMAN [continuing]. Market it, and then, hopefully, you drive the market.

Mr. ADAMS. My security is better than his security, so——

Senator LIEBERMAN. So you should buy mine.

Mr. ADAMS. Exactly right.

Senator LIEBERMAN. Do you want to respond, Mr. Watson?

Mr. WATSON. Yes, sir. We do see market pressure to provide more secure products and that is why we do provide a whole range of them and everyone else is getting into that game, too.

Senator LIEBERMAN. Right. So that is happening now?

Mr. WATSON. It is happening. No. 1, demand from the market is speeding quality of service. No. 2 is security, and that may switch. We do not know. There is a great enabler that security brings to freedom of use of the Internet economy.

Senator LIEBERMAN. Say a little more about this other part of it, the other side, that some foreign manufacturers are putting in gaps, vulnerabilities in the system that they can then penetrate. Is that being done by them for private gain or is it being done by their governments or what is happening?

Mr. ADAMS. If you look at the way, to take just 2, China and France, see the opportunity of the virtual space, they see this as no different from the terrestrial environment and there is a blurring, unlike in the United States, between the public and private sector. So what the Nation does, it does on behalf of the private sector.

It was striking when I was in Moscow a couple of years ago talking to their intelligence people and their sort of security folks in the prime minister's office. They were obsessed by what they felt were American attacks in the virtual space. So any equipment they bought from overseas, computer software, hardware, they felt had bugs of one kind or another planted in it.

Senator LIEBERMAN. That U.S. manufacturers had put in it?

Mr. ADAMS. Yes. Now, I have no idea whether that is true or not. What we do know is that other countries are very aggressively, indeed, contacting the United States, both with their impregnated devices of one kind or another and attacking through the virtual space. The challenge that we have is that we still see the front line as a Nation as soldier/sailor/airman/marine, our border. The front line actually is the private sector, because as you were rightly saying earlier, who is going to attack a soldier? You are actually going to attack the power grid or the telecom or you are going to steal the national intellectual property, and how easy it is because we do not actually understand the threat.

The awareness among CEOs or CIOs in the private sector and, indeed, in the public sector, is lamentable, and yet the threat and the way the America's technological advantage, and the fact that we are the most wired Nation in the world, is being exploited on a daily basis is a national outrage, and yet here we are.

Senator LIEBERMAN. Is there any way for a purchaser of a software system with a bug in it to determine that there is a bug in it as they use it?

Mr. ADAMS. You can, but it is very difficult. It is rather—I would say that there needs to be some way of a dialogue taking place between the traditional defenders of the nation-state, the intelligence community, the early warning system——

Senator LIEBERMAN. Right.

Mr. ADAMS [continuing]. And those that are in the front line and need to be defended. There is intelligence. There is information. There are things that you can do, but the degree of sharing of that knowledge is very, very limited indeed currently.

Senator LIEBERMAN. One of the things that strikes me, and you referred to it in a way, is that not only would a hostile power or group think about striking at purely private systems, but governmental systems and military systems even use private communication lines to convey information so that there is vulnerability in different ways. So what you just said is very important: There is more electronic interdependence of public sector and private sector than we generally acknowledge, and, therefore, a true solution to this security problem really has to be joint.

Mr. ADAMS. That is right, and if you think about how we traditionally see the nation-state, we see it as the government and the private sector goes on and does its thing and helps the nation-state when war breaks out. In the virtual space, war is going to be a constant. It is no different, if you like, to the way we were with terrorism in the early 1970s, when Congress would have hearings about bombings and assassinations and the bombers and assassins could choose the time and place and the target. We were very undefended. We did not understand the problem.

This is very similar to that, except the targeting has changed. The methods have changed. We are moving everything to the virtual space and the same actors are out there. It is just that we do not yet understand how to manage it, and it will be a comprehensive thing. There is no single fix. It is a series of things, some of them being done by Cisco with some of the excellent things that they make, some of them being done with the public-private partnership, some of them being driven by leadership that is going to come from people like yourselves.

Senator LIEBERMAN. Very interesting. As you both know but I think a lot of people out there do not know, it was the Federal Government, certainly through DARPA and the Defense Department, that did some of the initial work that led to the Internet and to the whole information revolution. Now, of course, we have fallen behind, certainly in this computer security part of it, behind the private sector that we in government gave birth to or spawned.

Do you have any ideas for what we might do to help government both be a stimulator, an incentivizer of more sophisticated computer security technology? Or in a broader sense, thinking perhaps idealistically, what government can do to be a model itself, which it is not now, for computer security?

Mr. ADAMS. If I can give you one statistic first, 20 years ago, 70 percent of all technology development was funded one way or another in America by the American Government. Today, that is under 5 percent. So in a single generation, you had an absolute transfer of energy, drive, and power from public to private. So what that says is that there needs to be—the public sector is never going to be a model. It cannot move fast enough. It is never going to be a zero-sum game. You are never going to get rid of the problem. You are only going to be able to effectively manage it.

So it is how to incorporate the private, how to see that the solution is outside and bring it in, rather than thinking about it being inside and imposing it out, and it is a very different way of thinking and a very radical way of thinking for government in its whole, because government in its whole tends to think that I am the answer, and in this case, that is not it.

Senator LIEBERMAN. I also serve on the Armed Services Committee. While this is not the perfect model and it is the minority of what happens, there is a lot more willingness to buy off-the-shelf today. In fact, some of our major defense systems are being built in a way that allows parts to be pulled out and the newest parts from the private sector to be put in over time, and maybe that is a model for computer security, as well.

Mr. Watson, do you want to respond?

Mr. WATSON. Yes, sir. First of all, it is true that the Internet knows no boundaries. There are no more perimeters, no more borders. It is all cyberspace.

Two things, though. Industry tends to develop things at Internet speed and move a lot faster than most governments can move. Since industry owns and operates most of the infrastructures on which the government, both private government and the infrastructures that we run, depend, it is our responsibility to do our part to develop solutions and we are doing that.

Also, in our studies, we have discovered that you can spend a lot of time studying the threat, but it is a lot more profitable to look at vulnerabilities and solve those to raise the bar of security. So that is the direction that we are taking. We are looking at vulnerabilities and addressing those. That is why it is important to do security posture assessments, risk assessments, to look at where you are and to know what you can fix at zero or little cost, as the NASA IG said.

Two provisions of the S. 1993 bill, I think, are really important. One is that it does include security as an integrated part, component, of each agency's business model and it emphasizes training as essential. That is a multi-faceted problem. Training security specialists is something we need to do and training everybody in the awareness problem and how users can better exercise security is important.

Senator LIEBERMAN. Should we be building on the DARPA model? Although again, maybe the private sector is zooming so far ahead that we do not have to do that. But there are certain areas in which, over time, we have found that because of market pressures, the private sector may not invest enough in research and development and so the government gets involved to do that. Is this an area where we ought to be targeting more Federal money in R&D and computer security breakthroughs?

Mr. WATSON. Before we will know the answer to that, it is important to have some kind of a clearinghouse and finding out what industry is doing, what academia is doing, what the government could target its money so it is not duplicating efforts. And I think the vehicle that we have in place right now, it is just a beginning, is the Partnership for Critical Infrastructure Security, and maybe the PCIS recommendation for the Institute for Information Infrastructure Protection might be able to be that clearinghouse.

Senator LIEBERMAN. Right.

Mr. ADAMS. I also think, though, that the way of—you take the DARPA model——

Senator LIEBERMAN. Right.

Mr. ADAMS [continuing]. You speak to folks at DARPA now, as you, I am sure, know, they focus not so much on inventing the new but integrating what is there, a different thing. Private industry is moving very, very rapidly. Cisco invests more money in thinking about new stuff on securing the Web than the government could ever really get together.

Senator LIEBERMAN. So maybe there is not a need for us to do it if the market is driving it.

Mr. ADAMS. But maybe there is a different way of doing it. I mean, what is there that the Federal Government can do to influence the outcome for the Nation? Education is fundamentally important. We go home at night, we unlock the door. We leave in the morning, we turn on the burglar alarm, we look the door, we make sure the windows are shut, and so on.. Nobody is being trained in these elementary things.

There is an enormous amount that could be done in education in schools, in universities, in funding programs, seed money that would ensure the security of the Nation going forward into this century rather than looking at, well, we have put in a spot of money here, but instead thinking about this in a national context. What is the best for the Nation as a whole that we, the Federal Government, can facilitate, because the private sector is continuing again to drive this revolution. So education is extremely important. Awareness is extremely important. And this is a major national security issue, so there are things that can be done from the Federal down to the local level.

Senator LIEBERMAN. Thank you both. You have been excellent witnesses. I appreciate your time.

Mr. WATSON. Thank you.

Chairman THOMPSON. Could I ask, just very briefly, how would you sell that from a national security standpoint? We talk about educating the young people and bridging the gap between the rich and the poor and all that, but how would you articulate the necessity to do that from a national security standpoint? These are kids. They are obviously going to use it in the short-term for things other than that. But from a long-term national benefit, are there not going to be just specialists that do that sort of thing? For the masses, it is certainly beneficial and maybe necessary, but does it really have to do with national security?

Mr. ADAMS. I would not posture it quite like that. Let me give you a brief anecdote. I was in a meeting about national security, American national security, a little while ago talking about future threats, 5 to 10 years. There was general agreement that China is a very significant threat to the United States.

At that same meeting, one of America's leading high-technology companies, they had one of their senior officers there and he was describing how they have had to make an investment decision about a new technology product that they are making, a new next step in the revolution. This is an American company. Where do we go? We go to the place where there is a customer base, where we have cheap labor and we have a high number of engineers. Where do they build their new factory? China. National security is irrelevant.

So the argument is not national security. The argument is what is going to be the resource for America in this century. Answer, trained and qualified people who can manage and master the revolution. As part of that, as part of that education process, just as you get trained in sanitation or good health practices, so you get trained in good security practices. It is part of being trained as an information specialist.

Chairman THOMPSON. In order to remain in a leadership position in the global economy, you have to maintain the productivity and, therefore, maintain your technological advantages, and, therefore, you have to have the educational background.

Mr. ADAMS. Exactly, and that is something that the government can absolutely influence the outcome of.

Chairman THOMPSON. What kind of group was this that you said you just attended?

Mr. ADAMS. I would have to talk to you about that outside.

Chairman THOMPSON. All right.

Mr. WATSON. I would suggest incentives to collaborate with the private sector. Cisco networking academies are in all 50 States and 25 foreign countries. We are adding security modules into that training. We build security training syllabuses and training partners deliver that training. We would view Federal requirements for security training as a market pressure and we would develop products and services to meet that demand.

Chairman THOMPSON. Mr. Watson, in your background with regard to information warfare, do you subscribe to the notion I have heard some say that it is almost for sure that in any future military attack, one industrialized country against another, that it would probably be preceded by a cyber attack?

Mr. WATSON. I would say that was possible and maybe even likely.

Chairman THOMPSON. What would you think, Mr. Adams?

Mr. ADAMS. I would say that most countries that have an information warfare capability see that as a precursor to full-scale war, and indeed, the full-scale war itself may occur in the virtual space. The interesting thing is that while America has a capability in this area, the lawyers have not yet decided what is war in the virtual space. So we may be attacked and in serious trouble before we can do anything about it.

Chairman THOMPSON. One final thing. Senator Lieberman and you mentioned the shift of capability from the government to the private sector and now we are here in our legislation trying to decide what government should be doing, first of all, about itself and managing itself. You heard the GAO testimony about the government needing to decide minimum standards.

I am wondering what is going on in the private sector out here. How is that going to interface with what we are trying to do? Should the government be setting standards for itself, minimum standards and as it is purchasing the hardware, software, servicing, and all from the outside, or should these be private standards determined by the private sector that we incorporate? Do you see what I am trying to get at? How does that interrelate?

Mr. ADAMS. I think there are two different things that you are addressing. What we have at the moment as this revolution has unfolded is a multitude of standards—hardware, software, different in America, different in Britain, different in France, all over the world.

Yes, it is a common arena, as Ken was saying earlier, and for the government or governments, more likely, the World Trade Organization to agree on a common standard is completely unrealistic, I think. It would take years and just will not happen.

More likely will be if you go back to the housing problems at the beginning of this century in the United States, a tremendous amount of poor housing that were in very bad shape. Nobody could agree what to do about it, but when the insurance industry said, OK, here is a minimum standard or else you do not get insurance. If you do not have insurance, you cannot have a mortgage. Lo and behold, the standards raised up and the standards of housing went up with it. The market drove the solution, in other words, and I think exactly the same thing will happen here.

There has been lots of talk about minimum risk standards and that needs to be applied. Two things will drive it. One will be down value chains. You are going to do business with me, you need to be affirmed at this risk level of some kind or another, certified at this risk level, and if you do not, then I am not going to do business with you.

And the second will be the insurance industry, which will say, if you are going to be insured with me, just like if I issue you with a house insurance policy, you get 10 percent off for this burglar alarm, 15 percent off if you are connected to the police station, so it will be a similar thing in the virtual space. So those two market factors will drive it.

Chairman THOMPSON. So instead of the government requiring certain standards of private industry, private industry would be requiring certain standards from the government?

Mr. ADAMS. Exactly.

Mr. WATSON. And we are already working in that direction. We are beginning to dialogue with the insurance and audit industries to develop standards. There are no standards across the board for security posture assessments or penetration tests or white-hat hacking or whatever you want to call it. If you ask two companies to give you an assessment of your security, you will get two completely different answers because they are based on different standards.

There is no standard training program for network security engineers to certify that someone has the skill required to do that kind of an assessment. There are no standard ratings for security in a network. How would you do that anyway? It would be an instantaneous security state, but how would you say, if you have a firewall, you have one level of standard. If you have a firewall, intrusion detection, and remote monitoring, you meet another security standard that could be insurable. Those are the kinds of questions that we need to address.

Chairman THOMPSON. Well, you know the GAO has these best practices and so forth. Do we not have any minimal standards, without being so minimal that they are meaningless?

Mr. WATSON. They are just not defined yet.

Mr. ADAMS. And there is no common language, we all speak—it sounds similar, but we all interpret it differently and you can give yourself a tick in the box which actually you are nowhere near where you should be.

Chairman THOMPSON. Thank you very, very much. We appreciate it.

Senator LIEBERMAN. Thank you.

Chairman THOMPSON. The record will remain open for 1 week after the close of the hearing. We are adjourned.

[Whereupon, at 12:50 p.m., the Committee was adjourned.]

APPENDIX

Prepared Statement of Kevin Mitnick

Honorable Chairperson Thompson, Distinguished Senators, and Members of the Committée:

My name is Kevin Mitnick. I appear before you today to discuss your efforts to create legislation that will ensure the future security and reliability of information systems owned and operated by, or on behalf of, the federal government.

I am primarily self-taught. My hobby as an adolescent consisted of studying methods, tactics, and strategies used to circumvent computer security, and to learn more about how computer systems and telecommunication systems work.

In 1985 I graduated cum laude in Computer Systems and Programming from a technical college in Los Angeles, California, and went on to successfully complete a post-graduate project in designing enhanced security applications that ran on top of a computer's operating system. That post-graduate project may have been one of the earliest examples of "hire the hacker:" the school's administrators realized I was hacking into their computers in ways that they couldn't prevent, and so they asked me to design security enhancements that would stop others' unauthorized access.

I have 20 years experience circumventing information security measures, and can report that I have successfully compromised all systems that I targeted for unauthorized access save one. I have two years experience as a private investigator, and my responsibilities included locating people and their assets using social engineering techniques.

My experience and success at accessing and obtaining information from computer systems first drew national attention when I obtained user manuals for the COSMOS computer systems (Computer Systems for Mainframe Operations) used by Pacific Bell.

Ten years later the novel "Cyberpunk" was published in 1991, which purported to be a "true" accounting of my actions that resulted in my arrest on federal charges in 1988. One of the authors of that novel went on to write similarly fictionalized "reports" about me for the New York Times, including a cover story that appeared July 4, 1994. That largely fictitious story labeled me, without reason, justification, or proof, as the "world's most wanted cybercriminal." Subsequent media reports distorted that claim into the false claim that I was the first hacker on the FBI's "Ten Most Wanted" list. That false exaggeration was most recently repeated during my appearance on CNN's Burden of Proof program on February 10, 2000. Michael White of the Associated Press researched this issue with the FBI, and FBI representatives denied ever including me on their "Ten Most Wanted" list.

I have gained unauthorized access to computer systems at some of the largest corporations on the planet, and have successfully penetrated some of the most resilient computer systems ever developed. I have used both technical and non-technical means to obtain the source code to various operating systems and telecommunications devices to study their vulnerabilities and their inner workings.

After my arrest in 1995, I spent years as a pretrial detainee without benefit of bail, a bail hearing, and without the ability to see the evidence against me, combined circumstances which are unprecedented in U.S. history according to the research of my defense team. In March of 1999 I pled guilty to wire fraud and computer fraud. I was sentenced to 68 months in federal prison with 3 years supervised release.

The supervised release restrictions imposed on me are the most restrictive conditions ever imposed on an individual in U.S. federal court, again according to the research of my defense team. The conditions of supervised release include, but are not limited to, a complete prohibition on the possession or use, for any purpose, of the following: cell phones, computers, any computer software programs, computer peripherals or support equipment, personal information assistants, modems, anything capable of accessing computer networks, and any other electronic equipment presently available or new technology that becomes available that can be converted to, or has as its function, the ability to act as a computer system or to access a computer system, computer network, or telecommunications network.

In addition to these extraordinary conditions, I am prohibited from acting as a consultant or advisor to individuals or groups engaged in any computer-related activity. I am also prohibited from accessing computers, computer networks, or other forms of wireless communications myself or through third parties.

I was released from federal prison on January 21, 2000, just 6 weeks ago. I served 59 months and 7 days, after earning 180 days of time off for good behavior. I am permitted to own a land line telephone.

Computer Systems and Their Vulnerabilities

The goal of information security is to protect the integrity, confidentiality, availability and access control to the information. Secure information is protected against tampering, disclosure, and sabotage. The practice of information security reduces the risk associated with loss of trust in the integrity of the information.

Information security is comprised of four primary topics: physical security, network security, computer systems security, and personnel security. Each of these four topics deserves a complete book, if not several books, to fully document them. My presentation today is intended to provide a brief overview of these topics, and to present my recommendations for the manner in which the Committee may create effective legislation.

1. Physical Security

1.1 Uncontrolled physical access to computer systems and computer networks dramatically increases the likelihood that the system can and will suffer unauthorized access.

1.1.1 Hardware Security

Computers may be locked in rooms or buildings, with guards, security cameras, and cypher-controlled doors. The greatest risk to information security in apparently secure hardware environments is represented by employees, or impostors, who appear to possess authorization to the secured space.

1.1.2 Data Security
Many government agencies require formal backup procedures to ensure against data loss. Equally stringent requirements must be in place to ensure the integrity and security of those backup files. Intruders who cannot gain access to secure data but who obtain unauthorized access to data backups successfully compromise any security measures that may be in place, and with much less risk of detection.

2. Network Security

2.1 Stand-alone computers are less vulnerable than computers that are connected to any network of any kind. Computers connected to networks typically offer a higher incidence of misconfiguration, or inappropriately enabled services, than computers that are not connected to any network. The hierarchy of network "insecurity" is as follows:
-- Stand-alone computer - least vulnerable
-- Computer connected to a LAN, or local area network - more vulnerable
-- Computer and a LAN accessible via dial-up - even more vulnerable
-- Computer and LAN connected to internet -- most vulnerable of all

2.1.1 Unencrypted Network Communications
Unencrypted network communications permit anyone with physical access to the network to use software to monitor all information traveling over the network, even though it's intended for someone else. Once a network tap is installed, intruders can monitor all network traffic, and install software that enables them to capture, or "sniff," passwords from network transmissions.

2.1.2 Dial-in Access
Dial-in access increases vulnerabilities by opening up an access point to anyone who can access ordinary telephone lines. Off site access increases the risk of intruders gaining access to the network by increasing the accessibility of the network and the remote computer.

3. Computer Systems Security

3.1 Computer systems that are not connected to any network present the most secure computing environment possible. However, even a brief review of standalone computer systems reveals many ways they may be compromised.

3.1.1 Operating Systems
The operating systems control the functions of the computer: how information is stored, how memory is managed, and how information is displayed -- it's the master program of the machine. At its core, the operating system is a group of discrete software programs that have

been assembled into a larger program containing millions of lines of code. Large modern day operating systems cannot be thoroughly tested for security anomalies, or "holes," which represent opportunities for unauthorized access.

3.1.2 Rogue Software Programs
"Rogue" software applications can be installed surreptitiously, or with the unwitting help of another. These programs can install a "back door", which usually consists of programming instructions that disable obscure security settings in an operating system and that enable future access without detection; some back door programs even log the passwords used to gain access to the compromised system or systems for future use by the intruder.

3.1.3 Ineffective Passwords
Computer users often choose passwords that are in the dictionary, or that have personal relevance, and are quite predictable. Static, or unchanging, passwords represent another easy method for breaching a computer system -- once a password is compromised, the user and the system administrators have no way of knowing the password is known to an intruder. Dynamic passwords, or non-dictionary passwords are problematic for many users, who write them down and keep them near their computers for easy access -- their own, or anyone who breaches physical security of the computer installation.

3.1.4 Uninstalled Software Updates
Out-of-date system software containing known security problems presents an easy target to an intruder. Systems administrators cannot keep systems updated as a result of work overload, competing priorities, or ignorance. The weaknesses of systems are publicized, and out-of-date systems typically offer well-known vulnerabilities for easy access.

3.1.5 Default Installations
Default installations of some operating systems disable many of the built-in security features in a given operating system. In addition, system administrators unintentionally misconfigure systems, or include unnecessary services that may lead to unauthorized access. Again, these weaknesses are widely publicized within the computing community, and default or misconfigured installations present an easy target.

4. Personnel Security

4.1 The most complex element in information security is the people who use the systems in which the information resides. Weaknesses in personnel security negate the effort and cost of the other three types of security: physical, network, and computer system security.

4.1.1 Social Engineering
Social engineering, or "gagging," is defined as gaining intelligence through deception. Employees are trained to be helpful, and to do what they are told in the workplace. The skilled social engineer will use these traits to his or her advantage as they seek to gain information that will enable them to achieve their objectives.

4.1.2 Email Attachments
Email attachments may be sent with covert code embedded within. Upon receiving the email, most people will launch the attachment, which can lower the security settings on the target machine without the user's knowledge. The likelihood of a successful installation using this method can be increased by following up the email submittal with a telephone call to prompt the person to open the attachment.

Information Security Exploits

Information security exploits are the methods, tactics, and strategies used to breach the integrity, confidentiality, availability or access control of information. Discovery of compromised information security has several consequences, the most important of which is the decline in the level of trust associated with the compromised information and systems that contain that information. Examples of typical security exploits follow.

5. Physical Security Exploits

5.1 Data Backup Exploit
Using deception or sheer bravado, the intruder can walk into the off site backup storage facility, and ask for the physical data backup by pretending to be from a certain agency. The intruder can claim that particular backup is necessary to perform a data restoration. Once an intruder has physical possession of the data, the intruder can work with the data as though he possessed superuser, or system administrator, privileges.

5.2 Physical Access Exploit
If an intruder gains physical access to a computer and is able to reboot it, the intruder can gain complete control of the system and bypass all security measures. An extremely powerful exploit, but one that exposes the intruder to great personal risk because they're physically present on the premises.

5.3 Network Physical Access Exploit
Physical access to a network enables an intruder to install a tap on the network cable, which can be used to eavesdrop on all network traffic. Eavesdropping enables the intruder to capture passwords as they travel over the network, which will enable full access to the machines whose passwords are compromised.

6. Network Security Exploits

6.1 Network software exists that probes computers for weaknesses. Once one system weaknesses are revealed and the system is compromised, the intruder can install software (called "sniffer" software) that compromises all systems on the network. Following that, an intruder can install software that logs the passwords used to access that compromised machine. Users routinely use the same or similar passwords across multiple machines; thus, once one password for one machine is obtained, then multiple machines can be compromised (see "Personnel Security Exploits").

7. Computer System Exploits

7.1 Vulnerabilities in programs (e.g., the UNIX program sendmail) can be exploited to gain remote access to the target computer. Many system programs contain bugs that enable the intruder to trick the software into behaving in a way other than that which is intended in order to gain unauthorized access rights, even though the application is a part of the operating system of the computer.

7.2 A misconfigured installation on a computer in operation at the Raleigh News and Observer, a paper in Raleigh, North Carolina, demonstrates the problematic aspect of system misconfiguration. Using the UNIX program "Finger," which enables one to identify the users that are currently logged into a computer system, I created a user name on the computer system I controlled. The user name I assigned myself matched exactly the user name that existed on the target host. The misconfigured system was set to "trust" any computer on the network, which left the entire network open for unauthorized access.

8. Personnel Security Exploits

8.1 Social Engineering -- involves tricking or persuading people to reveal information or to take certain actions at the behest of the intruder. My work as a private investigator relied heavily on my skills in social engineering.

In my successful efforts to social engineer my way into Motorola, I used a three-level social engineering attack to bypass the information security measures then in use. First I was able to convince Motorola Operations employees to provide me, on repeated occasions, the pass code on their security access device, as well as the static PIN. The reason this was so extraordinary is that the pass code on their access device changed every 60 seconds: every time I wanted to gain unauthorized access, I had to call the Operations Center and ask for the password in effect for that minute.

The second level involved convincing the employees to enable an account for my use on one of their machines, and the third level involved convincing one of the engineers who was already entitled to access one of the computers to give me his password. I overcame that engineer's vigorous reluctance to provide the password by convincing him that I was a Motorola employee, and that I was looking at a form that documented the password that he used to access his personal workstation on Motorola's network -- despite the fact that he never filled out any such form! Once I gained access to that machine, I obtained Telnet access to the target machine, access which I had sought all along.

8.2 Voice Mail and Fax Exploit
This exploit relies on convincing an employee at a large company to enable a voice mailbox: the intruder would call the people who administer the voice mailboxes for the target company and request a mailbox. The pretext would be that the intruder works for a different division,

and would like to retrieve messages without making a toll call.

Once the intruder has access to the voice mail system, the intruder would call the receptionist, represent himself as an employee of the company, and ask that they take messages for him; last but not least, the intruder would request the fax number and ask that incoming faxes be held for pickup. This sets the stage for the call to the target division of the company.

At this point, the intruder would call the target division to initiate the fax exploit with the goal of obtaining the targeted confidential company information. During that call the intruder would identify himself as an employee of the division whose voice mail and fax systems have just been compromised, he would cite the voice mail box in support of his identity, and would social engineer the target employee into faxing the target information to the compromised fax number located at one of their other offices.

Now the intruder would call the receptionist, tell the receptionist that he's in a business meeting, and ask that the receptionist fax the confidential material "to the hotel." The intruder picks up the fax containing confidential information at the secondary fax, which cannot be traced back to either the intruder or the targeted company.

I used this exploit to successfully compromise ATT's protected network access points routinely. ATT had learned that a system had been compromised by unauthorized entry at a central network access point called "DataKit." They imposed network access passwords on all DataKits to inhibit unauthorized access. I contacted one of the manager's secretaries and used the Fax Exploit to convince the secretary to fax me the password that enabled access to a DataKit that controlled dial-up access to ATT's worldwide computer network.

9. Recommendations

The Voice Mail and Fax Exploit demonstrates the most important element in my testimony today: that verification mechanisms are the weak link in information security, and voice mail and fax are the tools used to verify the authenticity of the credentials presented by someone seeking physical, network, or computer systems access.

The methods that will most effectively minimize the ability of intruders to compromise information security are comprehensive user training and education. Enacting policies and procedures simply won't suffice. Even with oversight the policies and procedures may not be effective: my access to Motorola, Nokia, ATT, Sun depended upon the willingness of people to bypass policies and procedures that were in place for years before I compromised them successfully. The corporate security measures that I breached were created by some of the best and brightest in the business, some of whom may even have been consulted by the committee as you drafted your legislation, Senate Bill S1993.

S1993 is represents a good first step toward the goal of increasing information security on government computer systems. I have several recommendations that I hope will increase the effectiveness of your bill.

1. Each agency perform a thorough risk assessment of the assets they want to protect.

2. Perform a cost-benefit analysis to determine whether the price to protect those systems represents real value.

3. Implement policies, procedures, standards and guidelines consistent with the risk assessment and cost benefit analyses. Employee training to recognize sophisticated social engineering attacks is of paramount importance.

4. After implementing the policies, procedures, standards and guidelines, create an audit and oversight program that measures compliance throughout the affected government agencies. The frequency of those audits ought to be determined consistent with the mission of a particular agency: the more valuable the data, the more frequent the audit process.

5. Create a numeric "trust ranking" that quantifies and summarizes the results of the audit and oversight programs described above. The numeric "trust ranking" would provide at-a-glance ranking -- a report card, if you will -- of the characteristics that comprise the four major categories defined above: physical, network, computer systems, and personnel.

6. Effective audit procedures -- implemented from the top down -- must be part of an appropriate system of rewards and consequences in order to motivate system administrators, personnel managers, and government employees to maintain effective information security consistent with the goals of this committee.

Conclusion

Obviously a brief presentation such as the one I've made today cannot convey adequately the measures needed to implement effective information security measures. I'm happy to answer any questions that may have been left unanswered for any members of the Committee.

United States General Accounting Office

GAO

Testimony

Before the Committee on Governmental Affairs, U.S. Senate

For Release on Delivery
Expected at
10 a.m.
Thursday,
March 2, 2000

INFORMATION SECURITY

Comments on the Proposed Government Information Security Act of 1999

Statement of Jack L. Brock, Jr.
Director, Governmentwide and Defense Information Systems
Accounting and Information Management Division

GAO
Accountability * Integrity * Reliability

GAO/T-AIMD-00-107

Mr. Chairman and Members of the Committee:

I am pleased to be here to discuss S. 1993, the Government Information Security Act of 1999, which seeks to strengthen information security practices throughout the federal government. Such efforts are necessary and critical. Our work has shown that almost all government agencies are plagued by poor computer security. Recent events such as the denial of service attacks last month indicate the damage that can occur when an organization's computer security defenses are breached. However, Mr. Chairman, let me emphasize that the potential for more serious disruption is significant. As I stated in recent testimony, our nation's computer-based infrastructures are at increasing risk of severe disruption. The dramatic increase of computer interconnectivity, while beneficial in many ways, has provided pathways among systems that, if not properly secured, can be used to gain unauthorized access to data and operations from remote locations. Government officials are increasingly worried about attacks from individuals and groups with malicious intentions, such as terrorists and nations engaging in information warfare.[1]

S. 1993 provides opportunities to address this problem. It updates the legal framework that supports federal information security requirements and addresses widespread federal information security weaknesses. In particular, the bill provides for a risk-based approach to information security and independent annual audits of security controls. Moreover, it approaches security from a governmentwide perspective, taking steps to accommodate the significantly varying information security needs of both national security and civilian agency operations.

---

[1] *Critical Infrastructure Protection: Comments on the National Plan for Information Systems Protection* (GAO/T-AIMD-00-72, February 1, 2000).

Mr. Chairman, I would like to discuss how these proposals can lead to substantial improvements in federal agency performance in addressing computer security issues. In addition, I would like to raise two additional concerns—the need for better-defined control standards and centralized leadership—that, if addressed, could further strengthen security practices and oversight. These two concerns merit further attention as the Committee moves ahead with its work in this area.

INFORMATION SECURITY IMPROVEMENTS ARE URGENTLY NEEDED

Improvements in agency information security practices are sorely needed. Our October 1999 analysis of our own and inspector general audits found that 22 of the largest federal agencies were not adequately protecting critical federal operations and assets from computer-based attacks.[2] Highlighting attention to this problem over the past 12 months was the disruption of operations at some government agencies caused by the Melissa computer virus as well as a series of federal web site break-ins. As in past analyses, we concluded that addressing this widespread and persistent problem would require significant management attention and action within individual agencies as well as increased coordination and oversight at the governmentwide level.

Our most recent individual agency review of the Environmental Protection Agency (EPA), corroborated our governmentwide analysis.[3] Overall, we found that EPA's computer systems

---

[2] *Critical Infrastructure Protection: Comprehensive Strategy Can Draw on Year 2000 Experiences* (GAO/AIMD-00-1, October 1, 1999).

[3] *Information Security: Fundamental Weaknesses Place EPA Data and Operations at Risk* (GAO/T-AIMD-00-97, February 17, 2000).

and the operations that rely on these systems were highly vulnerable to tampering, disruption, and misuse. EPA's own records identified several serious computer incidents in the last 2 years that resulted in damage and disruption to agency operations. Moreover, our tests of computer-based controls concluded that computer operating systems and the agencywide computer network that support most of EPA's mission-related and financial operations were riddled with security weaknesses. EPA is currently taking significant steps to address these weaknesses. However, resolving EPA's information security problems will require substantial ongoing management attention since security program planning and management to date have largely been a paper exercise doing little to substantively identify, evaluate, and mitigate risks to the agency's data and systems. Any fixes made by EPA to address specific control weaknesses will be temporary until these underlying management issues are addressed.

EPA is not unique. Within the past 12 months we have identified significant management weaknesses and control deficiencies at a number of agencies that effectively undermine the integrity of their computer security operations.

- In August 1999, we reported[4] that pervasive weaknesses in Department of Defense information security continue to provide both hackers and hundreds of thousands of authorized users the opportunity to modify, steal, inappropriately disclose, and destroy sensitive DOD data. Among other things, these weaknesses impaired DOD's ability to control physical and electronic access to its systems and data; ensure that software running

---

[4] *DOD Information Security: Serious Weaknesses Continue to Place Defense Operations at Risk* (GAO/AIMD-99-107, August 26, 1999).

on its systems is properly authorized, tested, and functioning as intended; and resume operations in the event of a disaster.

- In May 1999, we reported[5] that, as part of our tests of the National Aeronautics and Space Administration's (NASA) computer-based controls, we successfully penetrated several mission-critical systems, including one responsible for calculating detailed positioning data for each orbiting spacecraft and another that processes and distributes the scientific data received from these spacecraft. Having obtained access, we could have disrupted ongoing command and control operations and modified or destroyed system software and data.

- In August 1999, an independent accounting firm reported[6] that the Department of State's mainframe computers for domestic operations were vulnerable to unauthorized access. Consequently, other systems, which process data using these computers, could also be vulnerable. A year earlier, in May 1998, we reported[7] that our tests at State demonstrated that its computer systems and the information they maintained were very susceptible to hackers, terrorists, or other unauthorized individuals seeking to damage State operations or reap financial gain by exploiting the department's information security weaknesses.

---

[5] *Information Security: Many NASA Mission-Critical Systems Face Serious Risks* (GAO/AIMD-99-47, May 20, 1999).

[6] *Audit of the Department of State's 1997 and 1998 Principal Financial Statements*, Leonard G. Birnbaum and Company, LLP, August 9, 1999.

[7] *Computer Security: Pervasive Serious Weaknesses Jeopardize State Department Operations* (GAO/AIMD-98-145, May 18, 1998).

- In October 1999, we reported[8] that serious weaknesses placed sensitive information belonging to the Department of Veterans Affairs (VA) at risk of inadvertent or deliberate misuse, fraudulent use, improper disclosure, or destruction, possibly occurring without detection. Such findings were particularly troublesome since VA collects and maintains sensitive medical record and benefit payment information for veterans and family members and is responsible for tens of billions of dollars of benefit payments annually.

Although the nature of operations and related risks at these and other agencies vary, there are striking similarities in the specific types of weaknesses reported. The following six areas of management and general control weaknesses are repeatedly highlighted in our reviews.

- ***Entitywide Security Program Planning and Management.*** Each organization needs a set of management procedures and an organizational framework for identifying and assessing risks, deciding what policies and controls are needed, periodically evaluating the effectiveness of these policies and controls, and acting to address any identified weaknesses. These are the fundamental activities that allow an organization to manage its information security risks cost effectively, rather than reacting to individual problems ad hoc only after a violation has been detected or an audit finding has been reported. Despite the importance of this aspect of an information security program, we continue to find that poor security planning and management is the rule rather than the exception. Most agencies do not develop security plans for major systems based on risk, have not formally documented

[8] *Information Systems: The Status of Computer Security at the Department of Veterans Affairs* (GAO/AIMD-00-05, October 4, 1999).

security policies, and have not implemented programs for testing and evaluating the effectiveness of the controls they rely on.

- *Access Controls.* Access controls limit or detect inappropriate access to computer resources (data, equipment, and facilities) thereby protecting these resources against unauthorized modification, loss, and disclosure. They include physical protections, such as gates and guards, as well as logical controls, which are controls built into software that (1) require users to authenticate themselves through passwords or other identifiers and (2) limit the files and other resources that an authenticated user can access and the actions that he or she can execute. In many of our reviews we have found that managers do not identify or document access needs for individual users or groups, and, as a result, they provide overly broad access privileges to very large groups of users. Additionally, we often find that users share accounts and passwords or post passwords in plain view, making it impossible to trace specific transactions or modifications to an individual. Unfortunately, as a result of these and other access control weaknesses, auditors conducting penetration tests of agency systems are almost always successful in gaining unauthorized access that would allow intruders to read, modify, or delete data for whatever purposes they had in mind.

- *Application Software Development and Change Controls.* Application software development and change controls prevent unauthorized software programs or modifications to programs from being implemented. Without them, individuals can surreptitiously modify software programs to include processing steps or features that could later be exploited for personal gain or sabotage. In many of our audits, we find that (1) testing procedures are undisciplined and do not ensure that implemented software operates as intended, (2)

63-639 00 - 3

implementation procedures do not ensure that only authorized software is used, and (3) access to software program libraries is inadequately controlled.

- ***Segregation of Duties.*** Segregation of duties refers to the policies, procedures, and organizational structure that help ensure that one individual cannot independently control all key aspects of a process or computer-related operation and thereby conduct unauthorized actions or gain unauthorized access to assets or records without detection. For example, one computer programmer should not be allowed to independently write, test, and approve program changes. We commonly find that computer programmers and operators are authorized to perform a wide variety of duties, thus providing them the ability to independently modify, circumvent, and disable system security features. Similarly, we have also identified problems related to transaction processing, where all users of a financial management system can independently perform all of the steps needed to initiate and complete a payment.

- ***System Software Controls.*** System software controls limit and monitor access to the powerful programs and sensitive files associated with the computer systems operation, e.g., operating systems, system utilities, security software, and database management systems. If controls in this area are inadequate, unauthorized individuals might use system software to circumvent security controls to read, modify, or delete critical or sensitive information and programs. Such weaknesses seriously diminish the reliability of information produced by all of the applications supported by the computer system and increase the risk of fraud, sabotage, and inappropriate disclosures. Our reviews frequently identify systems with insufficiently restricted access which makes it possible for knowledgeable individuals to disable or circumvent controls in a wide variety of ways.

- ***Service Continuity Controls.*** Service continuity controls ensure that critical operations can continue when unexpected events occur, such as a temporary power failure, accidental loss of files, even a major disaster such as a fire. For this reason, an agency should have (1) procedures in place to protect information resources and minimize the risk of unplanned interruptions and (2) a plan to recover critical operations should interruptions occur. At many of the agencies we have reviewed, we have found that plans and procedures are incomplete because operations and supporting resources had not been fully analyzed to determine which were most critical and would need to be restored first. In addition, disaster recovery plans are often not fully tested to identify their weaknesses. As a result, many agencies have inadequate assurance that they can recover operational capability in a timely, orderly manner after a disruptive attack.

Unfortunately, in addressing these problems, agencies often react to individual audit findings as they are reported, rather than addressing the systemic causes of control weaknesses—namely, poor agency security planning and management. S. 1993 recognizes that this approach is unworkable in today's environment.

S. 1993 PROPOSALS CAN LEAD TO IMPROVED INFORMATION SECURITY MANAGEMENT

S. 1993 starts with the basic premise that computer security can only work within agencies if a strong management framework is in place. The bill, in fact, incorporates the basic tenets of good security management found in our report on security practices of leading organizations prepared at your request in 1998.[9] The bill proposes improvements in three significant areas:

- following a risk-based approach to information security,
- performing independent annual audits of security controls, and
- approaching security from a governmentwide perspective taking into account the varying information security needs of both national security and civilian agency operations.

If effectively implemented, these proposals should help federal agencies improve their information security practices and considerably strengthen executive branch and congressional oversight.

The first improvement area would require a risk management approach to be implemented jointly by agency program managers and technical specialists. Instituting such an approach is important since agencies have generally done a very poor job of evaluating their information security risks and implementing appropriate controls. Moreover, our studies of public and

[9] *Information Security Management: Learning From Leading Organizations* (GAO/AIMD-98-68, May 1998).

private best practices have shown that effective security program management requires implementing a process that provides for

- assessing information security risks to program operations and assets and identifying related needs for protection,
- selecting and implementing controls that meet these needs,
- promoting awareness of risks and responsibilities, and
- implementing a program for routinely testing and evaluating policy and control effectiveness.

The key to this process is recognizing that information security is not a technical matter of locking down systems, but rather a management problem that requires understanding information security risks to program operations and assets and ensuring that appropriate steps are taken to mitigate these risks. Thus, it is highly appropriate that S. 1993 requires a risk management approach that incorporates these elements.

The second proposed improvement area is the requirement for an annual independent audit of each agency information security program. Individually, as well as collectively, these audits can provide much needed information for improved oversight by the Office of Management and Budget (OMB) and the Congress. Our years of auditing agency security programs have shown that independent tests and evaluations are essential to verifying the effectiveness of computer-based controls. Audits can also evaluate agency implementation of management initiatives, thus promoting management accountability. Moreover, an annual independent evaluation of agency information security programs will help drive reform because it will spotlight both the obstacles and progress toward improving information security, much like the financial statement audits required by the Chief Financial Officers Act of 1990.

Agency financial systems are already subjected to such evaluations as part of their annual financial statement audits. However, I would like to note that for agencies with significant nonfinancial operations, such as the departments of Defense and Justice, the requirement for annual independent information security audits would place a significant new burden on existing audit capabilities. Accordingly, making these audits effective will require ensuring that agency inspectors general have sufficient resources to either perform or contract for the needed work.

Third, S. 1993 takes a governmentwide approach to information security by accommodating a wide range of information security needs and applying requirements to all agencies, including those engaged in national security. Under current law, distinctions between national security systems and all other government systems have tended to frustrate efforts to establish governmentwide standards and to share information security best practices. S.1993 should help eliminate these distinctions and ensure the development of common approaches across government for the protection of similar risks, regardless of the agencies involved.

This is important because the information security needs of civilian agency operations and those of national security operations have converged in recent years. In the past, when sensitive information was more likely to be maintained on paper or in stand-alone computers, the main concern was data confidentiality, especially as it pertained to classified national security data. Now, virtually all agencies rely on interconnected computers to maintain information and carry out operations that are essential to their missions. While the confidentiality needs of these data vary, all agencies must be concerned about the integrity and the availability of their systems and data. It is important for all agencies to understand these various types of risks and take appropriate steps to manage them.

STRENGTHENING SECURITY CONTROL STANDARDS AND LEADERSHIP ALSO MERITS ATTENTION

While S. 1993 would update the current legislative framework for computer security, two important considerations not addressed in the bill--the need for better-defined security control standards and the need to clarify and strengthen leadership for information security across government--are critical to strengthening security practices and oversight. I would like to discuss these in more detail as they complement the goals of S. 1993 and could significantly enhance its provisions.

First, there is a need for better-defined security control standards. Currently, agencies have wide discretion in deciding what computer security controls to implement and the level of rigor with which they enforce these controls. However, as mentioned earlier, our audit work has shown that agencies have generally done a poor job of evaluating risks and implementing effective controls. Moreover, these audits have shown that agencies need more specific guidance on the controls that are appropriate for the different types of information that must be protected. Current OMB and National Institute of Standards and Technology (NIST) guidance is not detailed enough to ensure that agencies are making appropriate judgments in this area and that they are protecting the same types of data consistently throughout the federal community.

More specific guidance could be developed in two parts:

- A set of data classifications that could be used by all federal agencies to categorize the criticality and sensitivity of the data they generate and maintain. These classifications could range from noncritical, publicly available information requiring a relatively low level of protection to highly sensitive and critical information that requires an extremely high level of protection. Intermediate classifications could cover a range of financial and other important and sensitive data that require significant protection but not at the very highest levels. It would be important for these data classifications to be clearly defined and accompanied by guidelines regarding the types of data that would fall into each classification.

- A set of minimum mandatory control requirements for each classification. Such control requirements could cover issues such as (1) the strength of system user authentication techniques (e.g., passwords, smart cards, and biometrics) for each classification, (2) appropriate types of cryptographic tools for each classification, and (3) the frequency and rigor of testing appropriate for each classification.

We believe that requiring the development of these standards, particularly with minimum mandatory control requirements, is the most important addition that could be made to your legislation. More precisely defined standards will provide common measures that can guide agencies in developing needed controls and improve the consistency and value of audits and evaluations.

Second, there is a need for strong, centralized leadership for information security across government. Under current law, responsibility for guidance and oversight of agency information security is divided among a number of agencies, including OMB, NIST, the General Services Administration (GSA), and the National Security Agency. Other organizations are also becoming involved through the administration's critical infrastructure protection initiative, including the Department of Justice and the Critical Infrastructure Assurance Office. While some coordination is occurring, overall, this has resulted in a proliferation of organizations with overlapping oversight and assistance responsibilities. Lacking is a strong voice of leadership and a clear understanding of roles and responsibilities.

Having strong, centralized leadership has been critical to addressing other governmentwide management challenges. For example, vigorous support from officials at the highest levels of government was necessary to prompt attention and action to resolving the Year 2000 problem. Similarly, forceful, centralized leadership was essential to pressing agencies to invest in and accomplish basic management reforms mandated by the Chief Financial Officers Act. To achieve similar results in information security, the federal government must have the support of top leaders and more clearly defined roles for those organizations that support governmentwide initiatives. We believe serious consideration should be given in your legislation to clarify the roles of organizations responsible for governmentwide information security efforts, for example, the roles of OMB, NIST, and GSA and to create a national Chief Information Officer to provide higher visibility and more effective central leadership of information security.

-- -- -- -- --

In conclusion, we support S. 1993. It provides ingredients essential to reforming agency information security practices and governmentwide oversight. In particular, it recognizes the highly networked nature of the federal computing environment; it calls for a more comprehensive, risk-based framework toward information security management; and it provides for annual independent audits of security programs. Basically, the bill provides a better management framework for addressing information security issues and provides a mechanism for independently checking how those issues are being addressed. As we noted, this objective could be further strengthened by requiring better-defined security control standards and strengthening governmentwide leadership.

Mr. Chairman and Members of the Committee, this concludes my testimony. We look forward to working with the Committee to advance the issues discussed today as well as to address our technical comments, which we have provided separately. I would be happy to answer any questions you may have.

(511184)

Statement of

ROBERTA L. GROSS
Inspector General

NATIONAL AERONAUTICS AND SPACE ADMINISTRATION

Before the

Senate Committee on Governmental Affairs

Mr. Chairman and members of the Committee,

I thank you for the opportunity to be here today to discuss S. 1993, the Government Information Security Act of 1999. My testimony generally will be based on the audits, reviews and criminal investigations performed by the NASA Office of Inspector General (OIG). This work provides insight into NASA's information technology (IT) security program. I also head a legislative working group reviewing S. 1993 comprised of OIG representatives from both the President's and Executive Councils on Integrity and Efficiency (PCIE/ECIE).[1] The group has received input from 24 members of these Councils. These representatives by and large agree that the S. 1993 is a very positive step in highlighting the importance of centralized oversight and coordination in responding to risks and threats to IT security. I will also offer comments raised by this group.

Introduction

At its most extreme, the interoperability of networks has made both our nation's and our agencies' critical infrastructures more vulnerable to intrusion and destruction. Consider NASA OIG's recent press release reporting on a joint computer crimes investigation by the NASA OIG
Computer Crimes Division (CCD); the Defense Criminal Investigative Service; the Federal Bureau of Investigation; the U. S. Department of the Interior, Office of Inspector General; and the Immigration and Naturalization Service, Office of Investigations.

> On February 23, 2000, Ikenna Iffih was charged in a three-count criminal information filed in U. S. District Court in Boston... Iffih obtained unauthorized

[1]Executive Order No. 12805, Integrity and Efficiency in Federal Programs, May 11, 1992, established the PCIE and ECIE. These Councils are chaired by the Deputy Director for Management of the Office of Management and Budget (OMB) and are comprised of Federal agency Inspectors General (IGs). IGs meet regularly to identify, review, and discuss areas of weakness and vulnerabilities to fraud, waste, and abuse in Federal programs.

access to a dial-up Internet account. On April 10-11, 1999, Iffih used that account to compromise a Defense Logistics Agency (DLA) computer in Columbus, OH. Using the DLA computer, Iffih illegally accessed a computer owned by the Zebra Marketing Online Service (ZMOS) in Seattle, WA, and through his allegedly reckless actions, damaged that computer and caused a significant loss of revenue to ZMOS. On May 6, 1999, Iffih illegally accessed a computer located at the Goddard Space Flight Center (GSFC) in Greenbelt, MD, and used his access to install a "sniffer" program to review and capture login names and passwords transmitted on the GSFC network. Iffih then used the GSFC computer to illegally access and modify (deface) a Department of the Interior web server on May 31, 1999.

On August 25, 1999, a search warrant was executed at Iffih's residence and the subsequent forensic examination of Iffih's personal computer revealed that Iffih had obtained unauthorized access to multiple computers owned and operated by Northeastern University (NEU), Boston, MA, and was in possession of personal identifying information on over 9,000 individuals associated with NEU.

Other recent headlines have made clear the vulnerability of our networked systems to malicious hackers. No one can doubt that securing information from theft, manipulation, denial of service attacks, and alteration will be an important factor in shaping future Federal planning and investment of information resources. However, determining how much security is enough is ultimately a matter of judgment. In a world of limited budgets and competing programmatic and infrastructure priorities, each agency must determine the most critical programs and the proper security for the systems supporting those programs. For example, NASA's mission includes inspiring the public through human exploration of space. The Space Shuttle, NASA's reusable space launch vehicle, piloted and staffed by its astronauts and principal investigators, is a key component of human space exploration. The shuttle program, including research projects conducted aboard the shuttle, involves elaborate network connectivity between the NASA centers and private industries, universities, and foreign nations. NASA also provides public web sites to inform the public about its role in the human exploration of space. Obviously, the level of security needed to protect NASA public web sites is not the same as that needed to ensure astronaut safety aboard the Space Shuttle.

Further complicating network security planning is that payback from the investment in information security is uncertain. Just recall discussions in the media as to whether the Y2K[2] effort was hype. However, headlines would have been far

[2]On February 4, 1998, the President issued Executive Order 13073, "Year 2000 Conversion," stating that, because of a design feature in many electronic systems, some computer systems and other electronic devices may misinterpret the date change to the year 2000. This flaw was labeled the "Y2K problem" because it could cause systems to compute erroneously or simply not run.

different if the Government's Y2K efforts had failed. IT security failures also make headlines.

Today's hearing reflects this Committee's recognition of the importance of planning a national coordinated approach to IT security. While it is essential that the debate continue over the precise implementation of a comprehensive plan, S. 1993 provides a good framework. Moreover, S. 1993 contemplates
that agencies will receive appropriate funding and personnel authority. IT security will not happen without appropriate funding and a core capability of skilled personnel. Nevertheless, there are current existing resources for effective controls ranging from guidance set forth in OMB Circular A-130[3] to the General Accounting Office's (GAO) various best practices guides, as well as the framework set forth in several recently enacted laws (e.g., Clinger-Cohen Act[4]). In addition, the Chief Information Officers (CIOs) individually and through their CIO Council have been studying and making recommen-dations in this arena. Also, various Inspectors General (IGs) have been active in providing recommendations through their reviews, audits and computer crimes investigations. One only needs to look through recent IG semiannual reports submitted to Congress to see the extensive activity by IGs in this arena. In the case of the NASA OIG, I refer you to our home page at http://www.hq.nasa.gov/office/oig/hq for the most recent semiannual report, as well as the full text of audits, reviews, and press releases of criminal investigations in the IT security arena.

Discussion of S. 1993

The proposed Act places responsibility on, accountability of, and coordination by some of the same players who made the Y2K readiness effort successful: OMB; the agency heads; the CIOs; GAO; and the IGs. In addition, because of the issues raised by information security, the Act also assigns specific roles to the Departments of Justice and Commerce, GSA, and law enforcement entities.

---

[3]OMB circular A-130 calls for a plan for adequate security of each general support system and major application as part of the organization information resources management planning process. The security plan shall be consistent with guidance issued by the National Institute of Standards and Technology (NIST). Independent advice and comment on the security plan shall be solicited prior to the plan's implementation. A summary of the security plans shall be incorporated into the strategic information resources management plan required by the Paperwork Reduction Act (44 U.S.C. Chapter 35) and Section 9(b) of the circular.

[4]The Clinger-Cohen Act of 1996 has established within Federal agencies the corporate framework for management of information resources, including both government information and information technology. The establishment of Chief Information Officers was singularly one of the most positive steps taken to focus attention on the management of information. Importantly, the Act called for a comprehensive information technology architecture that provides the integrated framework for both existing and newly acquired hardware and software.

Success of Y2K Coordinated Efforts Provides a Model for Similar Approach to IT Security

It is worthwhile to briefly look at the mobilization of the Federal government in addressing the Y2K problem. That effort highlights what agencies can accomplish when there is sufficient priority placed on an initiative by the President, OMB, agency heads, the CIOs, GAO, IGs, as well as the Congress in the exercise of its oversight authority. The Y2K readiness effort forced the government into strategic management of its information resources.

Determined to avert potential catastrophic collapse of critical infrastructures, the Federal, state and local governments, as well as the private sector, attempted to identify the mission criticality of individual systems only to find such distinctions blurred by network interdependencies. End-to-end testing performed to assess Y2K readiness became a time-consuming enterprise in defining the boundaries of networked environments. As the new millennium approached, the Federal government focused increased attention on the problem. The President appointed a Special Assistant, John Koskinen, Chair of the President's Council on Year 2000 Conversion; the Congress initiated focussed oversight on agencies' readiness; OMB required department and agency heads to submit detailed reports; agency heads made clear the mandate to their staffs to place this effort as a high priority; and IGs and the GAO devoted substantial resources and efforts to help ensure that their agencies were going to be ready when the date changed. The focus worked: We entered the new millennium with minimal Y2K problems.

As discussed below, S. 1993 also assigns responsibilities to these same players (as well as additional entities) and gives each a responsibility for the success of information security.

Roles Set Forth in S. 1993

OMB: The proposed bill gives wide latitude to OMB to take any authorized actions, including involving the budget or appropriations management process to enforce agency accountability for information resources. OMB will be required specifically to oversee and develop policies, principles, standards and guidelines for the handling of Federal information and information resources and to use its budgetary authority to enforce the accountability of the agency heads for information resources management and investments. Of course, OMB generally has these budgetary and policy authorities and has provided agencies considerable guidance (e.g., OMB Circular A-130). However, the explicit requirements emphasize the importance the Congress places on this effort. It re-emphasizes the mandate for OMB to hold agency heads accountable to implement information security and investment securities. Further, the Deputy Director for Management of OMB, to whom the Director may delegate the responsibilities under this proposed legislation, has a unique vantage point to coordinate efforts across the government by virtue of his/her role as Chair of the President's Management Council (PMC)[5]; the PCIE/ECIE; Chief Financial Officer[6] and CIO Councils initiatives. Planning responsibility at the Deputy Director level emphasizes to agency heads the importance placed on this initiative by the Congress.

Heads of Agencies: The agency heads occupy the "bully pulpit." They set the priorities of the Federal government by their personal involvement. It happened in the Y2K effort. It needs to happen in the IT security effort. This involvement means far more than issuing a memo or series of memos. The agency heads have to make clear that the current agency cultures, which permit very simple and avoidable vulnerabilities to occur and reoccur, are no longer acceptable.

Agency heads also have to ensure that their agency has sufficient trained personnel, a key requirement of the Act. Under the proposed Act, agency heads involvement extends to ensuring key officials (the CIO and senior program managers) perform their substantive responsibilities.

CIOs: The Act assigns considerable responsibility to CIOs for developing and maintaining agency information security programs, including assisting senior program managers in their responsibilities. The PCIE/ECIE working group noted that it would be helpful if the Act or legislative history provides greater guidance on the senior program manager function since that term is not defined in the proposed Act or existing legislation. Some agencies might view the position as a very senior high level official; others, as the individual in charge of a specific program (e.g., Shuttle Program).

Requirements of the bill alone, however, will not ensure the CIOs' success. Most participants in the PCIE/ECIE working group felt that agency CIOs lacked the leverage and control of resources necessary to successfully develop, implement, and evaluate their agencies' information security programs. Some even expressed the opinion that their agencies' CIOs were, at best, "paper tigers." The proposed bill contemplates, and the group supports giving teeth to the position in order to ensure CIO responsibilities are effectively carried out. Congress will have to maintain oversight of the agencies' empowerment of their CIOs.

---

[5]President's memorandum, October 1, 1993, reprinted at 58 FR 52393, established the President's Management Council (PMC). The PMC consists of the Chief Operating Officers of all Federal departments and the largest agencies. The PMC provides leadership for the most important Government-wide reforms.

[6]Pursuant to 31 USC, Section 90, Chief Financial Officers are appointed or designated for major Federal agencies and are responsible for agency policies, guidelines, and procedures for budget and financial management functions.

At NASA, the OIG has repeatedly recommended increased authority for the CIO. The Agency CIO has a limited staff and extremely limited budget (usually funds are provided for certain one time only NASA-wide purchases). The 10 Centers each have their own CIOs who collaborate with, but do not report to the NASA CIO. The Center CIOs each report to their Center's management who define their budgets, write their performance evaluations and allocate their staff positions. At some Centers, IT security resides in the security office; at other centers, it resides in the CIO's office.

In the past, we have been critical of this organizational approach to security by consensus because it results in delayed issuance and implementation of policies and procedures. Compounding this organizational structure, NASA has intentionally decentralized the CIO responsibility for IT security, designating different centers as the "Centers of Excellence" for specific functions: Ames Research Center (California) for IT security; Kennedy Space Center (Florida) for one component of Communications Security (COMSEC)[7] (Central Office of Records for the safeguard and control of COMSEC material[8]) with overall COMSEC management maintained within the Security Management Office at Headquarters; Goddard Space Flight Center (Maryland) for network incident response; Glenn Research Center (Ohio) for IT security training; and Marshall Space Flight Center (Alabama) for firewalls. We question the effectiveness of decentralizing and fragmenting these functions. Consider for example NASA's designation of Ames as the Center of Excellence for IT security. Ames personnel can and do conduct research into technology solutions for various IT vulnerabilities. Moreover, Ames coordinates with the Center CIOs, at a minimum, during weekly telecons and extensive exchange of email communications. These are all important practices. However, this assignment of responsibility to Ames reduces NASA's ability to efficiently and effectively utilize the enormous resources for IT security concentrated in the Washington, DC, metropolitan area. For example, the following offices are all located in Washington, DC, or its environs:

- NASA, the CIO, as well as the Security Office in charge of classified information policies and procedures.
- NASA OIG Computer Crimes Division forensics and media analysis.
- NASA IT Security Council - quarterly meetings occur at Headquarters where NASA-wide issues impacting the funding, staffing and other IT

---

[7]COMSEC generally encompasses secure measures and controls taken to deny unauthorized persons information derived from telecommunications and ensures the authenticity of such telecommunications. Communications security includes crypto-security, transmission security, emission security, and physical security of COMSEC material. For example, COMSEC measures are applied to protect the command and control communication links with the space shuttle.

[8]COMSEC Central Office of Records (COR): the NASA COR provides centralized management and control of all COMSEC material held by NASA COMSEC accounts. NASA COR responsibilities include: establishing and closing COMSEC accounts; and establishing or approving accounting procedures for accounts under its cognizance.

security issues are discussed (the Ames IT Security manager travels from Ames to attend this meeting or is connected by telecon).

- NASA's Automated Systems Incident Response Capability (NASIRC).
- National Security Counsel
- CIA
- NIST
- Department of Defense Joint Task Force – Computer Network Defense (JTF-CND)
- Department of Justice (DOJ) Computer Crimes and Intellectual Property Section (DOJ unit in charge of prosecuting network crimes).
- National Infrastructure Protection Center (NIPC)[9]

The NASA IT Security Manager could benefit by establishing close personal contacts with staff at the above listed agencies in order to stay current in their assessments of vulnerabilities, standards and best practices.[10] In the NASA OIG, we spend considerable time networking with these agencies to gain proficiency in IT security.

The proposed legislation requiring the CIO to designate a senior agency Information Security Officer will not address this decentralization at NASA. The Act does not require this position to report to the CIO, nor that this position be located in the CIO's office.

From our past work, we have seen very concrete examples where the decentralized structure weakened NASA's IT security posture. For example, NASA descoped the funding and responsibility NASIRC, a widely respected network incident response center, by fragmenting responsibility for its oversight at two centers, Ames (the Center of Excellence for IT security) and Goddard (the Center of Excellence for response). The Goddard Contracting Officer and Contracting Officer Technical Representative (COTR) performed oversight. Moreover, Centers differed widely in reporting intrusions to NASIRC. The absence of full reporting impacted the ability of the NASIRC to "connect the dots", to see the pattern of intrusions, and thereby, perhaps to discern the intent of the hackers and to prepare proper advice and warnings to the NASA Centers. The failure to report incidents also materially impacted on the ability of NASA OIG Computer Crimes Division (CCD) to be able to discern the pattern of criminal intent identify those conducting malicious attacks against NASA's systems. Because of these issues, my inspections unit conducted an assessment and made 11 recommendations to strengthen NASIRC. Management concurred, and we will conduct follow-up to ensure recommendations are fully implemented.

---

[9]See page 15-17 for a discussion of the NIPC's role in IT security.

[10]Moreover, it's been our experience that it is extremely difficult for Government to recuit and retain highly skilled computer professionals in the Ames area due to its high cost of living and proximity to California's Silicon Valley (San Jose).

Inspectors General (IGs): S. 1993 provides for responsibility of the IGs appointed under the IG Act of 1978 (5 U.S.C. App.) to perform annual evaluations and tests of the agencies' compliance with the IT security requirements of the Act. Alternatively, an independent auditor, as determined by the IG of the agency, can perform the annual evaluation requirements.

The PCIE/ECIE working group recommended that the Act apply to all IGs. As written, Presidentially appointed IGs created after the original Act of 1978 (e.g., the IG at Department of Justice) would not be included, nor would any ECIE IGs. The proposed change would also ensure that the IG of the agency would be the selecting official for the independent evaluator in all instances, not the head of the agency. The working group also commented that the outside reviewer should not be narrowly defined as an "independent external auditor" (implying a financial orientation), but instead, be any qualified external entity.

The PCIE/ECIE working group discussed the issue of the resources required for performing the annual review. To place their comments in context, I think it is instructive for the Committee to understand the OIGs' experience with the Chief Financial Officer (CFO) audits. The financial audit reports were annual and could be performed by the OIG or by an independent external auditor. In order to meet their requirements under the CFO Act, the OIGs dedicated substantial staff and budget.

In NASA's case, the Agency and OMB supported staffing increases (approximately 10 additional auditors) during the period the OIG performed the audit. Both the Agency and OMB's funding support and the CFO's substantial engagement enabled NASA to be one of the first Federal agencies to receive an unqualified opinion. Once NASA received two unqualified opinions from the NASA OIG, the Agency continued to support the CFO audit requirements by funding the external independent audit contract selected by the OIG. The OIG continued to dedicate staff to perform oversight of the contract, including the assurance that the independent audit met generally accepted government auditing standards.

Similarly, the annual report envisioned by the S. 1993 will require substantial personnel and budget commitment by each agencies' IG. In the case of the NASA OIG, information technology (IT) security has been one of the highest priorities of my office. The OIG currently has a robust program of criminal investigation, inspection, and audit activity focusing on protecting NASA's information resources and aggressively pursuing felonious intrusions resulting from hostile attacks on NASA information systems.

At the outset of my tenure, I was personally committed to building an IT audit, evaluation, and investigation IT security capability because of NASA's extensive dependence on network systems. In order to create the IT capabilities, I used vacancies created in other program areas. The Computer Crimes Division (CCD) is small, but smart and efficient.[11] Because I have recruited skilled staff for the computer crimes unit, they are usually at high grades; they are worth it.

The creation of the IT audit unit consisted of recruiting a handful of auditors and evaluators with some IT familiarity and training in-house auditors over the last four years. They began with very simple audits and received targeted training prior to each audit. They are now demonstrating increased skills, so they are able to perform more complex audits.

The office has made numerous recommendations to improve NASA's incident response capabilities and to protect sensitive technologies and other information from unauthorized access. For example, during an inspection, we uncovered security weaknesses involving data remaining on transferred and excessed personal computers.[12]

I have described the NASA OIG resource commitment so that the Committee will have a context to appreciate the comments on resources of the PCIE/ECIE working group. The reviews contemplated by S. 1993 will require recruiting, training and retaining a skilled set of personnel to perform the functions envisioned by the Act. The ability to perform the audits will be an evolving process. That also was the case for the CFO audits. Nevertheless, the investment in IT capability is well worth while for the oversight the IGs can provide and so should be supported by the agencies, OMB and the Congress through appropriate funding.

Law Enforcement Authorities: The Act provides that the CIO shall establish procedures for detecting, reporting, and responding to security incidents, including notifying and consulting with law enforcement officials and other offices and authorities. It also provides for notifying and consulting with an office designated by the Administrator of General Services within the General Services Administration.[13]

I want to address the CIO's requirements for "responding" and for "notifying law enforcement officials". The Act needs to make clear that the responsibility for

---

[11]As part of their efficiency and economy, the CCD forms prtnerships for tool development and share resources with entities such as the Department of Defense Computer Forensics Laboratory (DCFL). DCFL's mission includes providing digital evidence processing, analysis and diagnostics for DOD criminal, fraud, and counterintelligence investigations, operations and programs. We hope to continue forming partnerships with others in such areas as training.

[12]My office has published an instructional brochure on properly clearing data from hard drives, which I have previously provided for your information and use. This pamphlet was widely distributed throughout NASA and the IG community.

[13]The PCIE/ECIE working group could not comment about the GSA provisions because we were unsure which offices set forth in S. 1993 would perform the functions and responsibilities.

"responding" to security incidents does not includé "investigating" the incidents. Program officials by necessity have to perform some preliminary review in order to determine appropriate steps to protect critical systems and maintain operation and further analysis when they suspect potential crimes. However, systems administrators are not law enforcement investigators. The investigative role is reserved for special agents trained in evidence collection, chain-of-custody issues, and other legal issues impacting admissibly of evidence and court presentations.

The Act is silent as to what entities are meant by "law enforcement officials". Where an OIG has established a computer crimes division,[14] then the agency system administrators need to report to the IG special agents. It is crucial for the system administrators to work in close cooperation with special agents who can suggest alternatives to preserving evidence while minimizing impact on operations.

Of course, OIG special agents are not the only law enforcement officials involved in investigations of cyber crime. Presidential Decision Directive (PDD) 63 addresses the protection of critical infrastructures that include physical and cyber-based systems essential to the minimum operations of the economy and the government. As part of the protection of the nation's critical infrastructure, PDD 63 establishes the National Infrastructure Protection Center (NIPC) to, among other duties, "... serve as a national **critical** (bold in the original) threat assessment, warning, vulnerability and law enforcement investigation and response entity". The NIPC's role for critical infrastructure protection only reinforces the key role of Inspectors General to conduct investigation of agency network crimes. OIGs, because of their audit, inspection and investigative activity, are able to make key linkages about criminal activity and the need for better internal controls in their agencies. The legislative history of the IG Act makes this linkage one of the key reasons for creating OIGs.[15]

---

[14] Not surprisingly, more Inspectors General are establishing computers crime units as their agencies are more and more turning to e-commerce to conduct business, solicit grants and contracts and to purchase supplies. Investigators will no longer be able to rely on the "paper trail" to identify their suspect. They must be able to retrieve evidence stored in a computer and know how to properly seize a computer used in the commission of crimes.

[15]The IG Act specifically provides that the Offices of Inspector General were created to conduct and supervise investigations relating to the (Agency) programs and operations ..." of the Agency (Sec. 2).; " ...to conduct, supervise, and coordinate audits and investigations relating to the programs and operations .."of the Agency (Sec 4 (a)(1); and in carrying out the duties and responsibilities established under this Act, each Inspector General shall report expeditiously to the Attorney General whenever the Inspector General has reasonable grounds to believe there has been a violation of Federal criminal law" (Sec. 4 (d).

> [The OIG] provides a single focal point in each major agency for the effort to deal with fraud, abuse and waste in federal expenditures and programs. Without that focal point, the linkage between auditing and investigating is likely to be ineffective. ... Additionally this type of coordination and leadership strengthens cooperation between the agency and the Department of Justice in investigating and prosecuting fraud cases. The Department testified emphatically that those agencies which have been effective co-partners with the department have been those with viable offices of Inspector General.
>
> Senate report no. 95-1071, pp.2681-2682.

The Department of Justice has made clear that it does not contemplate that only the FBI has the authority to investigate or track computer offenses. Scott Charney, former Chief, Computer Crime and Intellectual Property Section, Department of Justice, wrote a letter dated February 1, 1997, to then Chair-Nominee of the President's Commission on Critical Infrastructure Protection. Mr. Charney stated:

> ... Second, I must correct the impression that at the federal level, only the FBI and the Department of Justice have the authority to investigate or track such attacks (computer offenses). Since 1984, when Congress passed the first computer crime statute, the U.S. Secret Service has had explicit jurisdiction over some kinds of computer crimes, along with the Federal Bureau of Investigation, which has general jurisdiction in this area. See 18 U.S.C., Sec 1030(d). In addition, many Federal agencies have criminal investigators with the training and the mission to investigate computer crimes directed against their own agencies. Some of these organizations, like the U.S. Air Force Office of Special Investigations, and the NASA Inspector General, have been leaders in this field.

As stated previously, IG special agents work closely with the Attorney General. The Department of Justice attorneys will function as the "honest broker", providing the proper coordination where IGs need to be working closely with the NIPC. The NIPC's focus is critical infrastructure. But there are thousands and thousands of daily intrusions. The NIPC does not investigate all of the thousands of agency intrusions because they are not all against the critical infrastructure. OIG special agents are the chief investigators for their victim agencies. The Act or report language should emphasize the important role of IGs in protecting their victim agencies.

CONCLUSION

In summary, the Act importantly recognizes that IT security is one of the most important issues in shaping future Federal planning and investment. By highlighting OMB's role, the Act recognizes that IT planning does not stop at the doorstop of any agency. By focusing on the roles of the agency heads and CIOs, the Act makes it clear that each agency must be far more vigilant and involved than current practices.

The IG community has already been involved in IT security oversight and criminal investigation of network intrusions. S.1993 provides an even greater role. This task will require IG commitment of staff and other resources. The agencies, OMB and Congress need to provide the leadership and budgetary support for all the key players the Act enlists to defend the nation's network systems.

Before the Senate Governmental Affairs Committee
"Protecting Federal Systems from Cyber Attack"
Mar. 2, 2000

Testimony of Kenneth Watson
Cisco Systems Inc.
Manager, Critical Infrastructure Protection

Chairman Thompson, Ranking Member Lieberman, distinguished members of the Senate, I appreciate the opportunity to speak with you today about network security best practices.

Cisco Systems is serious about network security, and about its implications for the critical infrastructures on which this and other developed nations depend. Cisco predicted that the Internet would change the way we work, live, play and learn. Just four years ago this was considered a bold statement, but today few would argue that the Internet is changing every aspect of our lives. The Internet economy is creating a level playing field for companies, countries and individuals around the world. In the 21st century, the big will no longer outperform the small – rather, the fast will beat the slow.

The Internet was originally built to share information among scientists and other researchers in a trusted academic environment. No one considered the need for information security or that its commercialization would proceed as rapidly as it has. Over the last 10 or 15 years, we have gradually become dependent on networks, not only for conducting electronic business, but also for delivery of vital goods and services, like electricity, communications, water, oil and gas, as well as controlling transportation and financial transactions. Network security solutions are equally applicable to both the private sector and government networks. While network protocols, vulnerabilities, countermeasures, and best practices are common, regardless of business sector, function, or mission, no two companies or federal departments will have the same requirements or optimum solutions at any given time. And those requirements and solutions will change over time.

So how do you decide on a "best practices" solution? Many companies have their own solutions, and in fact, the Federal Chief Information Officers Council is conducting a study to investigate best practices for federal departments and agencies. I would like to offer a simple way to organize network security technologies and practices, and talk a little about what Cisco has seen in customer networks.

There are many ways to organize security technologies and activities--it's important to choose one and then carry it out. Here is ours--it's called the "Security Wheel."

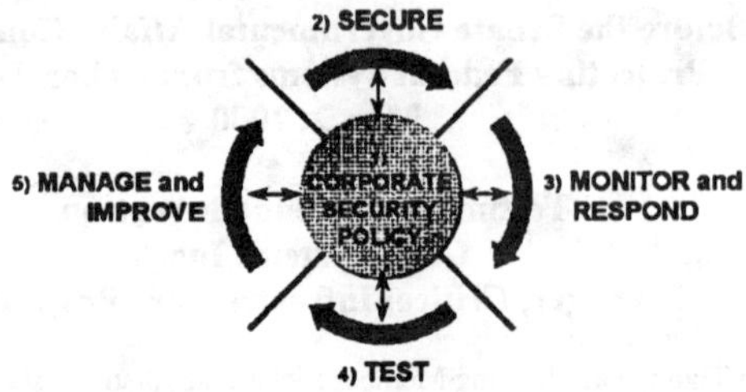

Figure 1. The Security Wheel

Good security must be based on policy. One of our teams was out installing an intrusion detection system, and the company CEO wanted a list of the top ten web sites visited by his employees. He was also in the process of buying a second T-1 line because of his company's increasing demand for bandwidth. We showed him that the top seven or so weren't related to his company's business--in fact, they were to sports scores, porn sites, etc. He was furious, and wanted names. "Heads will roll!" We advised him that the list represented a majority of his company, and he would do better to establish a simple web use policy. He sent a memo to all employees, showing the "top ten" list, and stating that browsing the web with company computers for non-business-related use would be restricted to before and after business hours and during lunch. This told his employees two things: he could see what they were doing, and he cared. Almost instantly, his need for a second T-1 vanished.

After setting appropriate policies, a company or organization must methodically consider security as part of normal network operations. This could be as simple as configuring routers to not accept unauthorized addresses or services, or as complex as installing firewalls, intrusion detection systems, centralized authentication servers, and encrypted virtual private networks.

A basic tenet of military combat engineers is that an unobserved obstacle will eventually be breached. The same is true in networks. Hackers will eventually figure out a way through or around static defenses. The number and frequency of computer attacks is constantly on the rise -- there are no "vacation periods." As such, a critical part of the security wheel is to monitor one's network infrastructure and then respond to attempted (or successful) attacks.

The next stop on the wheel is testing a network. Organizations should scan their own networks regularly, updating electronic network maps, determining what hosts and services are running, and cataloging vulnerabilities. They should also bring in experts to conduct independent network security posture audits once or twice a year to provide a more thorough assessment of vulnerabilities and to get independent, outside recommendations regarding countermeasures, security patches, and other improvements.

Finally, there must be a feedback loop in every "best practice." System administrators must be empowered to make improvements. Senior management must be held accountable for network security, and those involved in the day-to-day operations must have their attention. Only by collecting and managing appropriate network security data, through audit logs, intrusion detection and response systems, and network scans, can management make intelligent decisions and improve the network's security.

If you were to ask me what the most important step is, I would give you two answers: one for the short term, and one for the long term. In the short term, the best thing any company or government entity can do is to conduct a security posture assessment along with a risk assessment, to establish a baseline security state. Without measuring where you are, you can't possibly figure out where to go or how to get there.

Last week's issue of *Information Week* includes a report from our security consulting team on vulnerabilities we have seen while conducting security posture assessments in customer networks. We grouped vulnerabilities into three categories: denial of service, reconnaissance, and access. Denial of service vulnerabilities allow an outsider to block normal network traffic to a server. Reconnaissance vulnerabilities permit an attacker to gather information that may prove useful to a future attack. Access vulnerabilities allow attackers to alter or manipulate data in a network. I've attached some suggestions to this testimony for identifying and remedying the most common vulnerabilities, which apply to any network, public or private.

For the long term, the best thing we can do together is to close the alarming skills gap. The requirement for highly skilled security specialists is increasing faster than all the training programs combined can produce qualified candidates. Universities are having difficulty attracting both professors and students. The government is also having a hard time retaining skilled security specialists. We in the private sector are building and maintaining state-of-the-art security training programs, and we're collaborating with education institutions and training partners to provide a wide base for delivery. We're also helping the Office of Personnel Management to identify knowledge, skills, and abilities, ongoing training requirements, and career management and mentoring ideas for a Federal IT security workforce. This human resources issue is by far the most critical information security problem we face, and the solution must be based on government, industry, and academic collaboration.

This committee recently proposed new legislation to strengthen federal network security, S. 1993. Two provisions of this bill closely parallel what we in industry have been saying for some time: security must be promoted as an integral component of each agency's business operations, and information technology security training is essential to the success of any network security improvement program. Each department and agency should execute its own programs based on tailored mission and risk analyses.

Corporate network perimeters are blurring. That's also true for the lines between government and industry. The Internet knows no boundaries, and we're all in this together. We are very enthusiastic about the new Partnership for Critical Infrastructure Security, a voluntary organization of some 120 companies from across the country dedicated to improving the network security of our critical infrastructures. Already we have seen early fruits of this effort: 210 key executives attended a planning retreat here to begin to address interdependency vulnerabilities, information sharing, awareness and outreach, legislative and regulatory issues, research and development and workforce development. As we further build the relationship between the public and private sectors, we hope the great spirit of cooperation, led by the Department of Commerce and the Critical Infrastructure Assurance Office, will continue.

We will continue to work together to raise the bar of security overall, worldwide, so that we can empower our citizens and customers to take full advantage of the Internet economy in the Internet century.

I would be glad to take any questions.

Top Internet (External) and Intranet (Internal) Vulnerabilities and Recommended Fixes

This table outlines the vulnerabilities most often encountered by the Cisco Secure Consulting Services teams over the last six months. The vulnerabilities and their recommended fixes are applicable to any public or private Internet Protocol network.

[illegible]	
1. Internet	
A. Denial of Service	
Outdated, unnecessary network services (such as echo, chargen, systat, netstat)	Disable services as they are not typically required
Remote buffer overflow in the bootp network service	Disable bootp / disallow bootp access from the Internet. Bootp is a DHCP sub-service and there is no reason to run this service with access from the Internet
Remote buffer overflow in FTP network service	Update FTP server software to current release, apply security patches, enhance monitoring
B. Reconnaissance	
Portmapper provides RPC sub-service information	Disallow access to the RPC portmapper from the Internet
SMTP network services verify and expand	Update SMTP server software to current release, apply security patches, enhance monitoring
NFS network service allows remote users to obtain info on exports	Restrict access to the NFS server from the Internet
Statd RPC network service	Disable the service; disallow access to the statd service from the Internet
Cold Fusion web servers	Use configuration control on the web server, apply vendor patches, remove sample pages, enhance monitoring
C. Access	
Weak user authentication (default accounts, common accounts, joe accounts, null passwords)	Routine auditing of user selected passwords, password strength policy
SMTP mail relay	Update SMTP server software to current release; apply security patches, enhance monitoring.
Anonymous FTP access	Update FTP server software to current release, disable anonymous, apply security patches, enhance monitoring.
SMTP Pipe From	Update SMTP server software to current release, apply security patches, enhance monitoring.
SNMP Private community string	Change SNMP community names to something non-intuitive, disable access the SNMP from the Internet

[redacted]

2. Intranet	
A. Denial of Service	
Outdated, unnecessary network services (such as echo, chargen, systat, netstat)	Disable services as they are not typically required.
FTP pasv	Update FTP server software to current release, apply security patches, enhance monitoring.
Remote buffer overflow in the bootp network service	Disable bootp if not required, apply vendor security patches, enhance monitoring
Remote buffer overflow in FTP network service.	Update FTP server software to current release, apply security patches, enhance monitoring
B. Reconnaissance	
RPC Portmapper provides RPC sub-service information	Update RPC portmapper software, apply security patches, enhance monitoring
Finger provides username information	Disable the finger network service, apply vendor security patches, enhance monitoring
SMTP network services verify and expand	Update SMTP server software to current release, apply security patches, enhance monitoring.
Statd RPC network service	Disable the service, apply vendor security patches, enhance monitoring
SNMP public community string	Change SNMP community names to something non-intuitive, disable access the SNMP from the Internet
C. Access	
Weak user authentication (default accounts, common accounts, joe accounts, null passwords)	Routine auditing of user selected passwords, password strength policy
SMTP mail relay	Update SMTP server software to current release, apply security patches, enhance monitoring
SMTP Pipe From	Update SMTP server software to current release, apply security patches, enhance monitoring
SMTP Pipe To	Update SMTP server software to current release, apply security patches, enhance monitoring
SNMP Private community string	Change SNMP community names to something non-intuitive, disable access the SNMP from the Internet

TESTIMONY OF JAMES ADAMS
CHIEF EXECUTIVE OFFICER
INFRASTRUCTURE DEFENSE, INC.

COMMITTEE ON GOVERNMENTAL AFFAIRS
UNITED STATES SENATE

MARCH 2, 2000

Introduction
Chairman Thompson, Ranking Member Leiberman, members of the Committee, good morning and thank you for including me on this distinguished panel. My name is James Adams and I am the CEO of Infrastructure Defense Inc. (IDEFENSE).

By way of brief background, iDEFENSE provides intelligence-driven products -- daily reports, consulting and certification – that allow clients to mitigate or avoid computer network, Internet and information asset attacks before they occur. As an example, iDEFENSE began warning its clients about the possibility of Distributed Denial of Service attacks – the kinds of hacker activity that is currently capturing headlines across the globe - back in October and November of last year.

At the outset, I want to commend Senators Thompson and Lieberman, and their respective staff, for crafting such thoughtful and badly needed legislation in the area of computer security for the federal government. We are currently in the midst of a revolution, the Information Revolution, which calls for dramatic and bold steps in the area of securing cyberspace. The old ways of doing business don't work any more.

It is in this context that the Thompson-Lieberman bill takes a crucial step forward. By shaking up the current culture of lethargy and inertia gripping the federal government with a proposal to put teeth into the OMB's oversight of computer security issues this bill is a solid step in the right direction.

Why does this matter?

Few revolutions are accomplished without bloodshed. Already, as we plunge headlong and terribly ill-prepared into the Knowledge Age, we are beginning to receive the initial casualty reports from the front lines of the technology revolution and to witness first-hand the cyberthreats that, if allowed to fully mature, could cause horrendous damage to society.

The ongoing campaign of Denial of Service attacks include some of the household names of e-commerce — Microsoft, Yahoo, eBay, Amazon.com, CNN, ZDNet, and E*Trade. Comparative newcomer Buy.com was attacked on the day of its Initial Public Offering, and other smaller firms such as Datek Online Holdings Corp. experienced problems, which are probably related to the attacks. Targeted sites receive hits on their servers of up to one Gigabyte of data per second, and are unavailable to the general public for anywhere from 30 minutes to several hours.

From the headlines, you would think that these attacks suggested the end of the cyberworld as we know it. Nothing could be further from the truth. These were mere pinpricks on the body of e-commerce. Consider instead that some 30 countries have aggressive offensive Information Warfare programs and all of them have America firmly in their sights. Consider, to, that if you buy a piece of hardware or software from several countries, among them some of our allies, there is real concern that you will be buying doctored equipment that will siphon copies of all material that passes across that hardware or software back to the country of manufacture.

The hacker today isn't just the stereotypical computer geek with a grudge against the world because he can't get a date. And not every hack that is successfully pulled off is as sophomoric as, say, a recent incident when the self-styled Masters of Downloading hacked into the official U.S. Senate Web site and replaced its front page with a message proclaiming "Screw You Guys."

The hacker today is much more likely to be in the employ of a government, of big business or organized crime. And the hackers of tomorrow will be all of that and the disenfranchised of the 21st century who will resort to the virtual space to commit acts of terrorism far more effective than anything we've seen from the Armalite or the Semtex bomb in the 20th century.

Consider the band of Russian hackers who, over the past two years, have siphoned off an enormous amount of research and development secrets from U.S. corporate and government entities in an operation codenamed Moonlight Maze by American intelligence. The value of this stolen information is in the tens of millions—perhaps hundreds of millions—of dollars; there's really no way to tell. The information was shipped over the Internet to Moscow for sale to the highest bidder.

Fortunately, this threat was detected by a U.S. government agency. Unfortunately, that information was not passed on to the private institutions that it might have helped. Among government and industry alike, an understanding of the critical infrastructure's threat environment is barely in its infancy.

All of these attacks, mistakes, and plain acts of God need to be studied very carefully. Because they define the threat front that is driving right through our very fragile economic, governmental, and corporate armor.

These are the kind of problems we—jointly, the public and private sectors—face in the technology revolution. So the big question is, who is going to solve these problems? The government? Private industry? Or the two working together? Or are the problems going to be solved at all?

How has government responded so far? Well, there has been the usual President's Commission, and then the Principal's Working Group, then the bureaucratic compromise that nobody really wanted and then the National Plan which arrived seven months late and wasn't a plan at all but an invitation to have more discussions. Meanwhile, the government in all its stateliness continues to move forward as if the Revolution is not happening. Seven months ago, my company won a major contract with a government agency to deliver urgently needed intelligence. The money was allocated, the paperwork done. Yet it remains mired in the bureaucratic hell from which apparently it cannot be extricated. Meanwhile that same government agency is under cyber attack each and every day. This is not a revolution. This is business as usual.

Another government agency is trying to revolutionize its procurement processes to keep up with the pace of the revolution. They are proudly talking about reducing procurement times down to under two years. In other words, by the time new equipment is in place, the revolution has already moved on eight Internet years. In my company, if I can't have a revolutionary new system in place within 90 days, I don't want it.

What this means to me is that the threat is growing rapidly, that a largely inert government has so far been unable to meet the challenge and that more must be done. And this does matter because there is more at stake here than simply whether a new computer works or does not, whether a web site is hacked or not. At stake is the relationship between the governed and their government in a democracy. High stakes indeed.

So, I welcome the Thompson-Leiberman legislation as a good first step in the Senate efforts to try and control and drive the process that will bring the government up to speed with the revolution. I believe, however, that to effectively cope with the technology revolution, this proposal must be strengthened a great deal.

To fix the problems that afflict our body politic and our body corporate will require far more than Band-Aids. We're not talking casts and splints or even organ transplants. What we're talking about is leaving the old body and moving into a new one. We are talking—I am talking—about beginning to make changes in our cultural, political, and economic processes and institutions of such magnitude that they will dwarf even those that accompanied the industrial revolution.

What is needed is an outside entity – with real power – to implement drastic change in the way government approaches technology and the underlying security of its systems. Currently, jurisdictional wrangling, procurement problems and a slew of other issues are seriously hampering governments ability to stay current with the rapid pace of the Information Revolution. The Thompson-Lieberman bill provides a framework to begin sorting through this mess.

However, what is needed most is a person or an entity that will draw on skill sets in many areas will overlap that of the CIO, CFO, CSO, and most of the other officers or entities. Let's give this new person the title of Chief of Business Assurance. Or perhaps the Office of Business Assurance to relate it directly to the federal government.

This new acronym should be the response to the current need. In some ways it is mirrored by the debate that started at the beginning of the Information Revolution that led to the appointment of Chief Information Officers in many companies and within government. But Business Assurance is more than security, more than technology, and more than a combination of the two. It is an understanding of the whole environment and what that means for a business or a public sector operation.

The OBA's task would be to continuously gather and synthesize infrastructure-related trends and events, to intelligently evaluate the technological context within which the organization operates, to identify and assess potential threats, and then to suggest defense action. Or, viewed from the positive side, to assess the technological revolution's opportunities and propose effective offensive strategies.

The Office of Business Assurance must be a totally independent organization, with real teeth and power within government. Those organizations that have the foresight to create and properly staff this position will be immeasurably better equipped to handle the tidal wave of change that is just now beginning to break over our government, industry, economy, and culture.

There is much in common between government and industry when it comes to the challenges—and the opportunities—that the technology revolution poses. Both sectors face a common threat that ranges from vandal hackers and hard-core criminals to foreign agents and natural disasters. Both sectors share common goals for the well being of America and her people. Both employ technologies that are in essence identical. And both must work together to protect each other.

My company, Infrastructure Defense, pioneers an approach to infrastructure protection that is aimed chiefly at the private sector. Many of the principles, however—value-chain analysis, for example, and threat analysis—are directly transferable to government organizations. The two sectors are not that far apart.

With common problems and common goals, there are opportunities for common solutions. One of the most important, I believe—one that is too new to have been embraced by either the private or public sector—is the need for every organization to incorporate a risk-mitigation process. A second priority is to build a comprehensive information sharing system across all sectors on cyberthreats and countermeasures. We cannot afford to allow important information to grow stagnant within particular public or private entities. The rapid pace of technological change necessitates a correspondingly robust response mechanism. I urge this Committee to champion this important issue as the federal response to the growing cyberthreat is constructed.

Conclusion

I leave you with this thought. You will see total transformations of the way business and government is conducted, internally and externally. A failure to change to meet these new challenges is to risk the destruction that all revolutions bring in their wake. Proactive action is the route to survival.

We have heard a great deal in recent months about the potential of a digital divide that is developing between the computer haves and the computer have nots. I believe there is another digital divide that is growing between the American government and its citizens. If this Committee's efforts do not move forward in changing the culture of inertia, there is real danger that the "digital divide" that exists between the government and the private sector will only widen. We cannot afford a situation where the governed feel that their government is out of touch and increasingly irrelevant to their lives. By stepping up to the plate and tackling computer security with an innovative, bold approach the Thompson-Lieberman bill significantly boosts the chances of reversing the current bureaucratic approach to a dynamic problem.

Again, thank you for the honor of appearing before the Committee today.

II

106TH CONGRESS
1ST SESSION

S. 1993

To reform Government information security by strengthening information security practices throughout the Federal Government.

IN THE SENATE OF THE UNITED STATES

NOVEMBER 19, 1999

Mr. THOMPSON (for himself and Mr. LIEBERMAN) introduced the following bill; which was read twice and referred to the Committee on Governmental Affairs

---

A BILL

To reform Government information security by strengthening information security practices throughout the Federal Government.

Be it enacted by the Senate and House of Representatives of the United States of America in Congress assembled,

SECTION 1. SHORT TITLE.

This Act may be cited as the "Government Information Security Act of 1999".

SEC. 2. COORDINATION OF FEDERAL INFORMATION POLICY.

Chapter 35 of title 44, United States Code, is amended by inserting at the end the following:

"SUBCHAPTER II—INFORMATION SECURITY

"§ 3531. Purposes

"The purposes of this subchapter are to—

"(1) provide a comprehensive framework for establishing and ensuring the effectiveness of controls over information resources that support Federal operations and assets;

"(2)(A) recognize the highly networked nature of the Federal computing environment including the need for Federal Government interoperability and, in the implementation of improved security management measures, assure that opportunities for interoperability are not adversely affected; and

"(B) provide effective governmentwide management and oversight of the related information security risks, including coordination of information security efforts throughout the civilian, national security, and law enforcement communities;

"(3) provide for development and maintenance of minimum controls required to protect Federal information and information systems; and

"(4) provide a mechanism for improved oversight of Federal agency information security programs.

"§ 3532. Definitions

"(a) Except as provided under subsection (b), the definitions under section 3502 shall apply to this subchapter.

"(b) As used in this subchapter the term 'information technology' has the meaning given that term in section 5002 of the Clinger-Cohen Act of 1996 (40 U.S.C. 1401).

"§ 3533. Authority and functions of the Director

"(a)(1) Consistent with subchapter I, the Director shall establish governmentwide policies for the management of programs that support the cost-effective security of Federal information systems by promoting security as an integral component of each agency's business operations.

"(2) Policies under this subsection shall—

"(A) be founded on a continuing risk management cycle that recognizes the need to—

"(i) identify, assess, and understand risk; and

"(ii) determine security needs commensurate with the level of risk;

"(B) implement controls that adequately address the risk;

"(C) promote continuing awareness of information security risk;

"(D) continually monitor and evaluate policy; and

"(E) control effectiveness of information security practices.

"(b) The authority under subsection (a) includes the authority to—

"(1) oversee and develop policies, principles, standards, and guidelines for the handling of Federal information and information resources to improve the efficiency and effectiveness of governmental operations, including principles, policies, and guidelines for the implementation of agency responsibilities under applicable law for ensuring the privacy, confidentiality, and security of Federal information;

"(2) consistent with the standards and guidelines promulgated under section 5131 of the Clinger-Cohen Act of 1996 (40 U.S.C. 1441) and sections 5 and 6 of the Computer Security Act of 1987 (40 U.S.C. 759 note; Public Law 100–235; 101 Stat. 1729), require Federal agencies to identify and afford security protections commensurate with the risk and magnitude of the harm resulting from the loss, misuse, or unauthorized access to or modification of information collected or maintained by or on behalf of an agency;

"(3) direct the heads of agencies to coordinate such agencies and coordinate with industry to—

"(A) identify, use, and share best security practices; and

"(B) develop voluntary consensus-based standards for security controls, in a manner consistent with section 2(b)(13) of the National Institute of Standards and Technology Act (15 U.S.C. 272(b)(13));

"(4) oversee the development and implementation of standards and guidelines relating to security controls for Federal computer systems by the Secretary of Commerce through the National Institute of Standards and Technology under section 5131 of the Clinger-Cohen Act of 1996 (40 U.S.C. 1441) and section 20 of the National Institute of Standards and Technology Act (15 U.S.C. 278g–3);

"(5) oversee and coordinate compliance with this section in a manner consistent with—

"(A) sections 552 and 552a of title 5;

"(B) sections 20 and 21 of the National Institute of Standards and Technology Act (15 U.S.C. 278g–3 and 278g–4);

"(C) section 5131 of the Clinger-Cohen Act of 1996 (40 U.S.C. 1441);

"(D) sections 5 and 6 of the Computer Security Act of 1987 (40 U.S.C. 759 note; Public Law 100–235; 101 Stat. 1729); and

"(E) related information management laws; and

"(6) take any authorized action that the Director considers appropriate, including any action involving the budgetary process or appropriations management process, to enforce accountability of the head of an agency for information resources management and for the investments made by the agency in information technology, including—

"(A) recommending a reduction or an increase in any amount for information resources that the head of the agency proposes for the budget submitted to Congress under section 1105(a) of title 31;

"(B) reducing or otherwise adjusting apportionments and reapportionments of appropriations for information resources; and

"(C) using other authorized administrative controls over appropriations to restrict the availability of funds for information resources.

"(c) The authority under this section may be delegated only to the Deputy Director for Management of the Office of Management and Budget.

"§ 3534. Federal agency responsibilities

"(a) The head of each agency shall—

"(1) be responsible for—

"(A) adequately protecting the integrity, confidentiality, and availability of information and information systems supporting agency operations and assets; and

"(B) developing and implementing information security policies, procedures, and control techniques sufficient to afford security protections commensurate with the risk and magnitude of the harm resulting from unauthorized disclosure, disruption, modification, or destruction of information collected or maintained by or for the agency;

"(2) ensure that each senior program manager is responsible for—

"(A) assessing the information security risk associated with the operations and assets of such manager;

"(B) determining the levels of information security appropriate to protect the operations and assets of such manager; and

"(C) periodically testing and evaluating information security controls and techniques;

"(3) delegate to the agency Chief Information Officer established under section 3506, or a comparable official in an agency not covered by such section, the authority to administer all functions under this subchapter including—

"(A) designating a senior agency information security officer;

"(B) developing and maintaining an agencywide information security program as required under subsection (b);

"(C) ensuring that the agency effectively implements and maintains information security policies, procedures, and control techniques;

"(D) training and overseeing personnel with significant responsibilities for information security with respect to such responsibilities; and

"(E) assisting senior program managers concerning responsibilities under paragraph (2);

"(4) ensure that the agency has trained personnel sufficient to assist the agency in complying with the requirements of this subchapter and related policies, procedures, standards, and guidelines; and

"(5) ensure that the agency Chief Information Officer, in coordination with senior program managers, periodically—

"(A)(i) evaluates the effectiveness of the agency information security program, including testing control techniques; and

"(ii) implements appropriate remedial actions based on that evaluation; and

"(B) reports to the agency head on—

"(i) the results of such tests and evaluations; and

"(ii) the progress of remedial actions.

"(b)(1) Each agency shall develop and implement an agencywide information security program to provide information security for the operations and assets of the agency, including information security provided or managed by another agency.

"(2) Each program under this subsection shall include—

"(A) periodic assessments of information security risks that consider internal and external threats to—

"(i) the integrity, confidentiality, and availability of systems; and

"(ii) data supporting critical operations and assets;

"(B) policies and procedures that—

"(i) are based on the risk assessments required under paragraph (1) that cost-effectively reduce information security risks to an acceptable level; and

"(ii) ensure compliance with—

"(I) the requirements of this subchapter;

"(II) policies and procedures as may be prescribed by the Director; and

"(III) any other applicable requirements;

"(C) security awareness training to inform personnel of—

"(i) information security risks associated with personnel activities; and "(ii) responsibilities of personnel in complying with agency policies and procedures designed to reduce such risks;

"(D)(i) periodic management testing and evaluation of the effectiveness of information security policies and procedures; and

"(ii) a process for ensuring remedial action to address any deficiencies; and

"(E) procedures for detecting, reporting, and responding to security incidents, including—

"(i) mitigating risks associated with such incidents before substantial damage occurs;

"(ii) notifying and consulting with law enforcement officials and other offices and authorities; and

"(iii) notifying and consulting with an office designated by the Administrator of General Services within the General Services Administration.

"(3) Each program under this subsection is subject to the approval of the Director and is required to be reviewed at least annually by agency program officials in consultation with the Chief Information Officer.

"(c)(1) Each agency shall examine the adequacy and effectiveness of information security policies, procedures, and practices in plans and reports relating to—

"(A) annual agency budgets;

"(B) information resources management under the Paperwork Reduction Act of 1995 (44 U.S.C. 101 note);

"(C) program performance under sections 1105 and 1115 through 1119 of title 31, and sections 2801 through 2805 of title 39; and

"(D) financial management under—

"(i) chapter 9 of title 31, United States Code, and the Chief Financial Officers Act of 1990 (31 U.S.C. 501 note; Public Law 101–576) (and the amendments made by that Act);

"(ii) the Federal Financial Management Improvement Act of 1996 (31 U.S.C. 3512 note) (and the amendments made by that Act); and

"(iii) the internal controls conducted under section 3512 of title 31.

"(2) Any deficiency in a policy, procedure, or practice identified under paragraph (1) shall be reported as a material weakness in reporting required under the applicable provision of law under paragraph (1).

"§ 3535. Annual independent evaluation

"(a)(1) Each year each agency shall have an independent evaluation performed of the information security program and practices of that agency.

"(2) Each evaluation under this section shall include—

"(A) an assessment of compliance with—

"(i) the requirements of this subchapter; and

"(ii) related information security policies, procedures, standards, and guidelines; and

"(B) tests of the effectiveness of information security control techniques.

"(b)(1) For agencies with Inspectors General appointed under the Inspector General Act of 1978 (5 U.S.C. App.), annual evaluations required under this section shall be performed by the Inspector General or by an independent external auditor, as determined by the Inspector General of the agency.

"(2) For any agency to which paragraph (1) does not apply, the head of the agency shall contract with an independent external auditor to perform the evaluation.

"(3) An evaluation of agency information security programs and practices performed by the Comptroller General may be in lieu of the evaluation required under this section.

"(c) Not later than March 1, 2001, and every March 1 thereafter, the results of an evaluation required under this section shall be submitted to the Director.

"(d) Each year the Comptroller General shall—

"(1) review the evaluations required under this section and other information security evaluation results; and

"(2) report to Congress regarding the adequacy of agency information programs and practices.

"(e) Agencies and auditors shall take appropriate actions to ensure the protection of information, the disclosure of which may adversely affect information security. Such protections shall be commensurate with the risk and comply with all applicable laws.".

SEC. 3. RESPONSIBILITIES OF CERTAIN AGENCIES.

(a) DEPARTMENT OF COMMERCE.—The Secretary of Commerce, through the National Institute of Standards and Technology and with technical assistance from the National Security Agency, shall—

(1) develop, issue, review, and update standards and guidance for the security of information in Federal computer systems, including development of methods and techniques for security systems and validation programs;

(2) develop, issue, review, and update guidelines for training in computer security awareness and accepted computer security practices, with assistance from the Office of Personnel Management;

(3) provide agencies with guidance for security planning to assist in the development of applications and system security plans for such agencies;

(4) provide guidance and assistance to agencies concerning cost-effective controls when interconnecting with other systems; and

(5) evaluate information technologies to assess security vulnerabilities and alert Federal agencies of such vulnerabilities.

(b) DEPARTMENT OF JUSTICE.—The Department of Justice shall review and update guidance to agencies on—

(1) legal remedies regarding security incidents and ways to report to and work with law enforcement agencies concerning such incidents; and

(2) permitted uses of security techniques and technologies.

(c) GENERAL SERVICES ADMINISTRATION.—The General Services Administration shall—

(1) review and update General Services Administration guidance to agencies on addressing security

considerations when acquiring information technology; and

(2) assist agencies in the acquisition of cost-effective security products, services, and incident response capabilities.

(d) OFFICE OF PERSONNEL MANAGEMENT.—The Office of Personnel Management shall—

(1) review and update Office of Personnel Management regulations concerning computer security training for Federal civilian employees; and

(2) assist the Department of Commerce in updating and maintaining guidelines for training in computer security awareness and computer security best practices.

SEC. 4. TECHNICAL AND CONFORMING AMENDMENTS.

(a) IN GENERAL.—Chapter 35 of title 44, United States Code, is amended—

(1) in the table of sections—

(A) by inserting after the chapter heading the following:

"SUBCHAPTER I—FEDERAL INFORMATION POLICY";

and

(B) by inserting after the item relating to section 3520 the following:

"SUBCHAPTER II—INFORMATION SECURITY

"Sec.
"3531. Purposes.

and

(2) by inserting before section 3501 the following:

"SUBCHAPTER I—FEDERAL INFORMATION POLICY".

(b) REFERENCES TO CHAPTER 35.—Chapter 35 of title 44, United States Code, is amended—

(1) in section 3501—

(A) in the matter preceding paragraph (1), by striking "chapter" and inserting "subchapter"; and

(B) in paragraph (11), by striking "chapter" and inserting "subchapter";

(2) in section 3502, in the matter preceding paragraph (1), by striking "chapter" and inserting "subchapter";

(3) in section 3503, in subsection (b), by striking "chapter" and inserting "subchapter";

(4) in section 3504—

(A) in subsection (a)(2), by striking "chapter" and inserting "subchapter";

(B) in subsection (d)(2), by striking "chapter" and inserting "subchapter"; and

(C) in subsection (f)(1), by striking "chapter" and inserting "subchapter";

(5) in section 3505—

(A) in subsection (a), in the matter preceding paragraph (1), by striking "chapter" and inserting "subchapter";

(B) in subsection (a)(2), by striking "chapter" and inserting "subchapter"; and

(C) in subsection (a)(3)(B)(iii), by striking "chapter" and inserting "subchapter";

(6) in section 3506—

(A) in subsection (a)(1)(B), by striking "chapter" and inserting "subchapter";

(B) in subsection (a)(2)(A), by striking "chapter" and inserting "subchapter";

(C) in subsection (a)(2)(B), by striking "chapter" and inserting "subchapter";

(D) in subsection (a)(3)—

(i) in the first sentence, by striking "chapter" and inserting "subchapter"; and

(ii) in the second sentence, by striking "chapter" and inserting "subchapter";

(E) in subsection (b)(4), by striking "chapter" and inserting "subchapter";

(F) in subsection (c)(1), by striking "chapter, to" and inserting "subchapter, to"; and

(G) in subsection (c)(1)(A), by striking "chapter" and inserting "subchapter";

(7) in section 3507—

(A) in subsection (e)(3)(B), by striking "chapter" and inserting "subchapter";

(B) in subsection (h)(2)(B), by striking "chapter" and inserting "subchapter";

(C) in subsection (h)(3), by striking "chapter" and inserting "subchapter";

(D) in subsection (j)(1)(A)(i), by striking "chapter" and inserting "subchapter";

(E) in subsection (j)(1)(B), by striking "chapter" and inserting "subchapter"; and

(F) in subsection (j)(2), by striking "chapter" and inserting "subchapter";

(8) in section 3509, by striking "chapter" and inserting "subchapter";

(9) in section 3512—

(A) in subsection (a), by striking "chapter if" and inserting "subchapter if"; and

(B) in subsection (a)(1), by striking "chapter" and inserting "subchapter";

(10) in section 3514—

(A) in subsection (a)(1)(A), by striking "chapter" and inserting "subchapter"; and

(B) in subsection (a)(2)(A)(ii), by striking "chapter" and inserting "subchapter" each place it appears;

(11) in section 3515, by striking "chapter" and inserting "subchapter";

(12) in section 3516, by striking "chapter" and inserting "subchapter";

(13) in section 3517(b), by striking "chapter" and inserting "subchapter";

(14) in section 3518—

(A) in subsection (a), by striking "chapter" and inserting "subchapter" each place it appears;

(B) in subsection (b), by striking "chapter" and inserting "subchapter";

(C) in subsection (c)(1), by striking "chapter" and inserting "subchapter";

(D) in subsection (c)(2), by striking "chapter" and inserting "subchapter";

(E) in subsection (d), by striking "chapter" and inserting "subchapter"; and

(F) in subsection (e), by striking "chapter" and inserting "subchapter"; and

(15) in section 3520, by striking "chapter" and inserting "subchapter".

SEC. 5. EFFECTIVE DATE.

This Act and the amendments made by this Act shall take effect 30 days after the date of enactment of this Act.

○

GAO
Accountability * Integrity * Reliability

United States General Accounting Office
Washington, DC 20548

Accounting and Information
Management Division

B-285030

March 31, 2000

The Honorable Daniel K. Akaka
Committee on Governmental Affairs
United States Senate

Subject: Information Security: Posthearing Questions Concerning the Proposed Government Information Security Act of 1999

Dear Senator Akaka:

This letter responds to the March 6, 2000, letter from Ms. Hannah Sistare, Staff Director and Counsel of the Senate Committee on Governmental Affairs, requesting on your behalf that we answer several follow-up questions related to our March 2, 2000, testimony.[1] During that testimony, we discussed the proposals in S. 1993, the Government Information Security Act of 1999, which seeks to strengthen information security practices throughout the federal government. Your questions, along with our responses, follow.

Question 1 *Should we be concerned that national security programs may become more vulnerable as a result (of what S. 1993 would do)?*

Answer S. 1993 does not limit the extent to which agencies can protect their computer-supported operations, including those related to national security. Conversely, the bill emphasizes the importance of recognizing that highly critical and sensitive data and operations merit a higher level of security than those that are less critical and sensitive. S. 1993 would place responsibility for determining what levels of protection are appropriate for the various types of data and operations in the hands of agency program managers. As a result, managers of classified programs would be responsible for determining how to protect their classified data in accordance with their agencies' policies. In essence, S. 1993 provides a generic framework for improving

[1] *Information Security: Comments on the Proposed Government Information Security Act of 1999* (GAO/T-AIMD-00-107, March 2, 2000).

(1) agency management of information security and (2) oversight of agency practices. Such a framework can benefit all agency programs—both classified and unclassified—by helping to ensure that controls commensurate with risk are implemented effectively.

Question 1.a *How can we ensure under S. 1993 that both classified and unclassified information systems will be adequately protected?*

Answer S. 1993 provides for a risk-based approach to information security that requires agency managers to determine what levels of protection are appropriate and ensures that such protections are effectively implemented. Under this approach, classified systems would continue to be subject to security requirements applicable under existing agency policies, unless agencies determined that such requirements and related policies needed to be modified.

Question 1.b *Won't there be a tendency to focus on classified systems, perhaps slowing down the public's access to unclassified information?*

Answer S. 1993 recognizes that for security "one size does not fit all." Accordingly, the level of public access allowed would vary depending on the sensitivity of the information in question. Disclosure of some unclassified information is prohibited by law, such as sensitive taxpayer information. The protection of government information from unauthorized access is important due to national security and privacy concerns. Ensuring adequate protection of the data in no way affects the right of citizens to access public information through mechanisms, such as the Freedom Of Information Act, which was established to provide them access. S. 1993's focus on risk management is designed to accommodate all levels of data sensitivity.

Question 2 *Have we historically provided adequate guidance, oversight and funding to each executive department to enable them to effectively address current day vulnerabilities—or is that the crux of the problem?*

Answer While guidance, oversight, and funding have been provided, they have not kept pace with the quickly evolving computing environment over the last decade. In addition, audits have shown that agencies have done a poor job of implementing existing guidance. S. 1993 seeks to update and improve guidance to agencies and improve oversight by requiring annual evaluations of agency security programs.

Question 2.a *Is the current situation so dire that serious consideration of a national Chief Information Officer (CIO) is a logical step to take at this time?*

Answer Yes. As I mentioned in my testimony, information systems at most federal agencies are highly vulnerable to attack and misuse, and there is a need for stronger, more centralized leadership in this area. A federal CIO could help coordinate agency security activities and facilitate solutions for common problems. Concurrently, a federal CIO could benefit other aspects of information technology management, such as strategic planning, managing system investments, and software development. It is important that all of these aspects of information technology management, including information security, be managed under a cohesive strategy.

Please contact me at (202) 512-6240 if you have any questions. I can also be reached by e-mail at *brockj.aimd@gao.gov.*

Sincerely yours,

Jack L. Brock, Jr.
Director, Governmentwide and Defense
Information Systems

(511967)

National Aeronautics and
Space Administration
Headquarters
Washington, DC 20546-0001

MAR 31 2000

Ms. Hannah Sistare
Staff Director and Counsel
United States Senate
Committee on Governmental Affairs
Washington, DC 20510-6250

Dear Ms. Sistare:

Enclosed is our response to the additional questions posed by Senator Akaka from the March 2, 2000, hearing entitled "Cyber Attack: Is the Government Safe?"

Our office is committed to improving information security and adequately protecting NASA information technology resources. Because vulnerabilities to command and control operations of spacecraft are of great concern to the NASA Office of Inspector General, we have issued several reports related to command and control issues. We also have issued many reports on other NASA information security vulnerabilities. I would be glad to provide you briefings on these matters, at your convenience.

If you or your staff have any questions or need additional information regarding our response, please contact me at (202) 358-1220 or Mr. Alan Lamoreaux, IG Executive Officer, at (202) 358-2061.

Sincerely,

Roberta L. Gross
Inspector General

Enclosure

NATIONAL AERONAUTICS & SPACE ADMINISTRATION
MS. ROBERTA GROSS
INSPECTOR GENERAL

Responses to Questions for Panel 2
Senate Committee on Governmental Affairs
March 2, 2000 Hearing
Cyber Attack: Is the Government Safe?

Background:

The following quote is from the May 1999 GAO Information Security Report entitled Many NASA Mission-critical Systems Face Serious Risks. "With nothing more than publicly available Internet access, we performed penetration testing at one of NASA's 10 field centers, simulating outside attackers. Our test team was able to systematically penetrate systems involved in two mission critical functions: (1) supporting the command and control of spacecraft and (2) processing and distributing scientific data returned from space. The systems supporting the command and control of spacecraft were involved in determining and verifying a variety of detailed spacecraft positioning data, such as orbital attitude (the precise orientation of a spacecraft with respect to the earth) and other orbit information used in planning spacecraft maneuvers and establishing and maintaining communications with ground controllers. . . ."

Question 1: Are spacecraft command and control systems classified national security systems?

Answer: The spacecraft command and control systems are considered classified national security systems only if the mission contains a classified payload or if the mission involves classified national security information. In addition, command and control systems are classified if the information from the mission is used to augment national security operations in the event of a national emergency.

Question 2: What was the reason for such poor controls over such a critical system?

Answer: The controls and procedures in place to protect the critical systems were weak, in part, due to the absence of a robust information security program which lacks: adequate policies and procedures, adequately qualified information security professionals, appropriate program funding for security, and effective enforcement and follow-up to ensure compliance with applicable federal regulations.

Question 3: Have these problems been fixed?

Answer: **Agency-wide efforts are underway to address the problems, but significant problems remain (see response to questions 2). I would note that the penetration testing addressed in the GAO report involved ground-based computers used for command and control. It did not include radio-frequency based spacecraft commanding. Radio frequency based spacecraft commanding also requires adequate authentication regardless of whether the mission is national security related or purely commercial. In this area, NASA has not effectively implemented policy requiring approved communications security techniques be applied to NASA spacecraft.**

CISCO SYSTEMS

Cisco Systems, Inc.
12515 Research Blvd.
Austin, TX 78759
Phone: 512 249-8055
Fax: 512 249-8506
http://www.cisco.com

March 31, 2000

Chairman Fred Thompson & Senator Joseph Lieberman
Committee on Governmental Affairs
United States Senate
Washington, DC 20510-6250

Dear Senators Thompson & Lieberman:

Thank you for the opportunity to offer additional information pertinent to the March 2, 2000 hearing entitled "Cyber Attack: Is the Government Safe?" I hope the following adequately answers the committee's question as posed by Senator Akaka.

QUESTION:
Many believe that the private sector should and must take the predominant role in resolving the cyber network security problem. Do you share this view, and do you foresee the overall problem improving, or getting worse as technology evolves?

RESPONSE:
Cisco believes that the private sector should take the predominant role in resolving network cyber security challenges. However, the private sector needs and hopes to partner closely with government, combining our strengths and leveraging our core competencies to achieve network security. And separate and apart from industry efforts, the government clearly has responsibility for protecting government computers and networks from attack. We are confident that, working together, we can collectively address the challenges as technology evolves.

We believe that this public-private partnership is the most effective response to potential attacks. In the private sector, incentives must be put into place to encourage all network administrators to deploy security technologies to protect themselves and their customers from hacker attacks. In the public sector, we are grateful that the Federal Bureau of Investigation has devoted significant resources to investigating the recent denial of service attacks and we hope the perpetrators will be prosecuted to the fullest extent of the law. We also encourage the federal government to serve as a model for private industry by equipping its own computer networks with the best security measures possible.

1. The Private Sector Should Lead Efforts to Address Cyber Security Challenges

Going forward, it is clearly up to the private sector to assume the lead role in network security. Private sector leadership makes sense for several reasons, not the least of which is that the vast majority of networks are built, owned and operated by private industry. Market forces drive us to develop solutions quickly, with the aim of continued robust delivery of goods and services. In addition, the private sector brings several core competencies to bear, specifically:

- Market-driven solutions
- Operational expertise
- Robust investment in research and development
- The ability to respond quickly to changing market requirements
- State-of-the-art training and education programs
- Industry-driven standards

Private industry has indeed begun stepping up to the plate in just the past few weeks. Already, each of the private infrastructure sectors is organizing to address concerns raised by Presidential Decision Directive 63 and the National Plan for Information Systems Protection, Version 1.0, in cooperation with their government sector liaisons. The new Partnership for Critical Infrastructure Security is addressing cross-sector concerns, while providing a vehicle for private sector input into the national planning process and to the National Infrastructure Assurance Council as it develops advice for the President. We in the Partnership hope to more fully involve government leaders, the privacy community, and academia, and are taking steps to do so. Meanwhile, we have identified broad areas of mutual concern to both government and the private sector, and are planning on a formal organization with defined support and liaison relationships to expedite our work.

2. The Private Sector Needs and Hopes to Partner with Government to Secure our Networks

For the private sector to succeed, however, it will need a strong and engaged partner in government. Government brings several unique capabilities to the Partnership including:

- The ability to offer incentives for market-driven solutions beyond what due diligence and market pressure can provide.
- Power to remove barriers to information sharing (e.g. liability).
- Access to threat information for a better understanding of risk.
- A bully pulpit from which to wage a national education program.
- The ability to coordinate a national research and development agenda.

Sharing of information on threats and effective responses between private sector and government will be critical to our success.

3. Separate from Industry Efforts, Government Needs to Take Responsibility for its Own Systems.

Government will need to take the leading role with respect to protecting government systems, particularly military and national security networks. Government systems are uniquely attractive targets to hackers and contain uniquely critical data. In addition, the government must defend against third parties "hijacking" its powerful networks to attack others. We concur with the objectives stated by this Committee -- the federal government should strive to serve as a model for private industry by equipping its own computer networks with the best security measures possible.

4. Will the Problem Improve or Get Worse?

While short-term problems may increase, I believe that in the long term we can dramatically improve the state of network security by working together. To address short term challenges, data-driven management decisions can effect change. Security posture assessments can not only provide baseline security states of department, agency, and company networks, they can serve as awareness vehicles for senior management.

In the long term, we must invest in a national education and training program and conduct basic and applied security research. Industry and academia can build network security training programs, but must collaborate with the government on training requirements and standards. Coordinating university network security syllabi, re-training federal and private sector employees, and promoting corporate training programs should become a top agenda item. Building a reliable, secure, next generation Internet is possible if we meet research challenges together. New technologies like malicious code detection, mobile agents, and sensor technologies over IP could expedite long-term solutions. We won't know what combinations are needed until we invest in and conduct this research together.

I believe the Partnership for Critical Infrastructure Security represents a great beginning to the public-private collaboration needed to fully resolve our common infrastructure assurance problem. I look forward to working more closely with government, academia, and other industry partners as we empower our citizens and customers to take full advantage of the Internet economy in the Internet century.

Please contact me at (512) 378-1112 or e-mail: kwatson@cisco.com if you have additional questions.

Sincerely,

Ken Watson
Cisco Systems, Inc.